W9-BBH-750

The Make-It-Yourself Shoe Book

The Make-It-Yourself SHOE BOOK

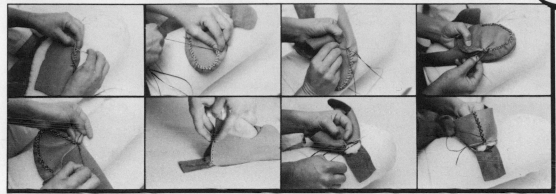

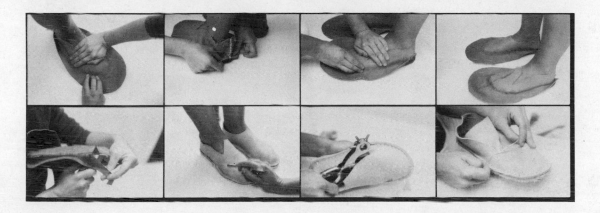

Christine Lewis Clark

ALFRED A. KNOPF   NEW YORK   1977

THIS IS A BORZOI BOOK
PUBLISHED BY ALFRED A. KNOPF, INC.

LIBRARY OF CONGRESS CATALOGING IN PUBLICATION DATA
Clark, Christine Lewis.   The make-it-yourself shoe book.
1. Books and shoes. I. Title.
TT678.5.C58   646.4   76-47933
ISBN 0-394-41057-2

MANUFACTURED IN THE UNITED STATES OF AMERICA
FIRST EDITION

Contents

Leather   4

Soling   10

Padding   14

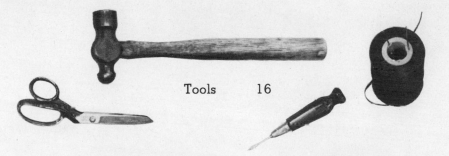

Tools   16

Feet   27

Moccasins   34

Shoes   57

Boots   77

Sandals   84

Acknowledgments

The information in this book was neither gained nor recorded in a vacuum. In its garnering, we are forever indebted to the hundreds of customers and students who were so patient and enthusiastic and enabled us to earn while we learned. In its recording, I sincerely thank Jerry Lynch for his generous rescue with the photography, Betty Cascio for her clarity in reading, and Nancy Nicholas of Knopf for everything. My parents, Harriet and Bill Lewis, deserve love and thanks for all their support during both periods.

The Make-It-Yourself Shoe Book

Introduction

The Make-It-Yourself Shoe Book is for anyone interested in the art and craft of handmaking shoes, sandals, moccasins, or boots for himself, his friends, his family, or for profit. The instructions in the book are a distillation of the information and techniques my partner Jim and I have gotten together over the years from our experience first as custom shoemakers and then as teachers of the craft. Everything has been carefully worked out and with this book anyone should be able to make at home, by hand, with a minimal investment in tools and materials and no costly machinery or equipment, his or her own durable, attractive, relatively inexpensive, and perfectly fitting footwear.

You will find instructions for three different types of footwear: shoes, moccasins, and sandals. In each section only one basic technique or pattern is given, with a few simple variations. Once you have mastered the fundamentals, you can vary the finished products to suit yourself—that is just a matter of taste. But the instructions for each design have been worked out very carefully to enable you to master the complexities of achieving a perfect fit, your most important goal. For instance, although the moccasin pattern is for the traditional Indian gathered-toe design, working with that pattern you can achieve anything from a simple baby's slipper to a hefty hiking boot. The sandals are all based on the continuous-strap technique because that has turned out to be the most comfortable as well as the most practical and versatile. And the innovation in *The Make-It-Yourself Shoe Book* you probably won't even notice unless you know something about shoemaking. It is that modern materials and methods of leather tanning have enabled us to work out a design for shoes that dispenses with the traditional last—a piece of wood shaped like a foot. This may seem like nothing to you but never before has there been a way of making a shoe directly over the foot. This means that the form you are molding your shoe over—your foot—is not only the most accurate but also the least expensive and the most readily available.

A quick flip through the pictures will show you that there is an enormous variety of styles available using just these three patterns and that you should be able to make shoes for any occasion or mood. I am assuming that you will be so delighted with your first pair that you will make many pairs of shoes over a number of years. At times the instructions may seem a bit more detailed than you may think you want for making your first pair, but as you progress you will find that all the information is necessary and that the finished product is worth the care and attention.

Custom shoemaking is a hobby that will give your mind and your hands something practical to do for a long time, and part of the pleasure you will get from it will come from refining your technique. Please don't feel you have failed if you cannot do everything perfectly on your first attempt. Remember these shoes are especially made for you from your own foot drawings and no mistake you could make can result in anything as potentially harmful as the fit of some of the sloppily made commercial shoes available. If your first efforts at stitching aren't as professional looking as you would like, relax; it will come. What you will have made is a shoe that fits perfectly—you have all the time in the world to make it look perfect as well.

With care and attention to detail and, above all, practice you will be able to turn out a shoe, sandal, or moccasin, a boot or a slipper that will not only feel superb but will have none of the crude look of so many handmade items. It will be a proud day for you when in answer to an admiring question you will be able to say, "I *made* them." I wish I could be there to share that day with you.

Leather

Leather is a highly sensuous material. We all love to feel it, see it, and smell it and look forward to working with it. Unfortunately, the subject of leather is vast. If you are going to make footwear, you cannot just go out and get some leather and start to work. What kind of leather will you get? Your wallet and your jacket are both made of thin leather, but they are not alike. Your belt and a saddle are both made of thick leather, but they are not alike. Talking about leather is probably boring for all of us; it is the working with it that we anticipate and enjoy. However, if you are to work with it and get the right kind to work with, I have to talk about it. I'll try to make it short.

ABOUT LEATHER

Since leather is the skin of animals and people like beef as a source of meat, it only follows that most of the leather available to you will be from the hide of a beef, or cowhide. Because leather is more popular today than ever before in history, the uses of cowhide have expanded immensely and the methods of tanning it for these uses have grown more and more sophisticated. Nowadays it is frequently difficult to recognize cowhide as cow. There are a thousand different ways it can look and feel. The processing or tanning of leather is highly involved: the skin goes through softening, cleaning, trimming, fleshing, dehairing, splitting, smoothing, flexing, oiling, ironing, tumbling, drying, dying, and painting before it appears on the shelf for sale. In selecting your leather it is important to have a vague understanding of some of these processes so you can discuss the subject intelligently. However, the mass of it is no more important to you as a consumer than the slaughtering and butchering process is to your selection of meat.

Cowhide

Obtaining suitable leathers of decent quality will by your biggest challenge in shoemaking. Your main sources will be leather supply houses, some shoe findings stores—who sell supplies to shoe repairers—and some tanneries if you are very, very lucky and they will sell to you. Assuming you will have to go through the supply houses, I'll work using their terminology and categories.

Cowhide has three qualities that will be important to you in your selection: (1) weight or thickness, (2) method of tanning, and (3) finish.

WEIGHT AND THICKNESS. Weight and thickness are synonymous. The thicker the leather, the more the hide will weigh. Hides are sold by the square foot for a certain price per foot. The weight is standardized by referring to the number of ounces a particular square foot of leather weighs. If a representative square foot weighs 2 ounces, for example, it is called 2-ounce leather. Because it can vary in thickness throughout the hide, ounces are discussed in such ranges as 2–3 ounces, or 4–6 ounces, or 8–9 ounces. Below is the standard chart for thickness per ounce: that is, a leather weighing 2 ounces will be exactly that thick. Weight goes higher than 10, but for all practical purposes you will not be buying anything thicker.

Cows do not conveniently grow up with hides nicely divided into thick-skinned and thin-skinned. The raw or "green" hide is very thick, sometimes as much as ½ inch. Depending upon the intended use, the tanner might put these very thick hides through a process known as splitting. The hide is peeled/split/cut into several layers. The part of the hide

Thickness Chart

Weight of leather is designated in ounces.
This scale shows the relative thickness
of the various weights.

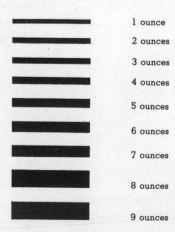

▬▬▬▬	1 ounce
▬▬▬▬	2 ounces
▬▬▬▬	3 ounces
▬▬▬▬	4 ounces
▬▬▬▬	5 ounces
▬▬▬▬	6 ounces
▬▬▬▬	7 ounces
▬▬▬▬	8 ounces
▬▬▬▬	9 ounces

that was on the outer part of the body, holding the hair, is called the top grain. The underlayers are called splits. The top grain is the quality layer and the only layer you should use in shoemaking. Splits are fuzzy on both sides, and because they were not the tough outer portion they are weak and inferior. Although sometimes quite pretty, they tear (which leather should never do), are difficult to work with, and generally are used in cheap clothing and shoes. If you are about to buy something commercially and it is "sueded," be certain to look inside the garment to see if the other side is top grain or is also "sueded." If the inside is fuzzy too, it means they are passing off a split on you and it will not hold up well. It is no deal.

When the tanner gets the hide he cuts it in half, because the full cowhide is enormous and too difficult to work with. Therefore, in discussing a hide, we are really discussing half of the cow, a side. A small hide or side will run about 14 square feet and a large one about 25 square feet. The footage is measured by the tanner on a special machine.

The thickest portion of the hide comes from the back or shoulder of the animal. This thickest part can be cut into a rectangle, called a bend, and used for soling. The rest of the "whole" (half) hide is split into desired thicknesses.

After you have felt various hides, your hands will start telling you this is 2 ounces, this is 6 ounces, etc. Very approximately, garment leather is from 1 to 4 ounces, "our" shoe and moccasin leather is from 4 to 7 ounces, and sandal leather from 6 to 10 ounces.

TANNING METHOD. We speak of hides in terms of the materials or substances used to process the

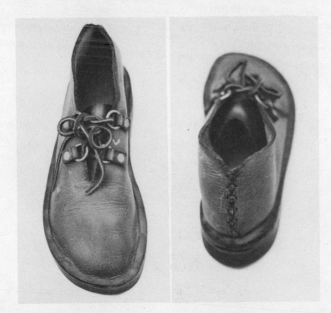

leather. Tanning leather with vegetables is the oldest process. Traditionally the bark of the oak tree was used, and thus such leather can be called oak-tanned or bark-tanned or vegetable-tanned. This leather looks pink or flesh-colored. If there is a "natural" color of leather, this is it—pink. To my knowledge, there is no pretty tan or brown leather which is natural. Everything is bleached or dyed or colored during the processing. Vegetable-tanned leather can come in any thickness, but generally it runs fairly heavy; it is porous and can be soaked in water, molded, and will dry in the molded shape. Saddles are made this way. Anything termed bridle leather, harness leather, a belt slab, or belly leather is completely unsuitable for the uppers of shoes or moccasins. It is much too stiff, has no oil content, and will dry out and crack if it is used on a sandal unless you oil it heavily. This is the leather that is used for tooling and stamping, as it holds the impression when it has been wetted. I only use it for midsoling when I can obtain a cheap belly hide.

Latigo. Latigo is a leather that has been heavily permeated with oil by the tanner. The top side feels smooth and oily, the way you think good leathery leather should feel. It is usually thought of as being heavy leather, although I have seen it as thin as 5 ounces. It takes dye well and evenly, it's easy to work with, and does not crack or stiffen up when used for a sandal. It cannot be soaked in water and molded, although it can be stamped and tooled. It was frequently used in belts, sandals, and the heavy bags that were so popular in the late sixties. I rarely use it except for sandals. As with most leathers, some latigos, such as "western" latigos, are superior to others and cost accordingly. Latigo is completely unsuitable for our moccasins, because it is too stiff to gather. I have made shoes of latigo, although it presented enormous problems in molding because of the high oil content and the stiffness. Don't start with latigo shoes; work up to them, if you try them at all, when you know what you are doing.

One form of latigo is called teal and is dripping with oil. This is a soft and pliable leather, good for work boots and shoes to be worn in rainy areas, but extremely difficult to work with because the oil keeps the glue from adhering.

Chrome-tanned leather. Chrome tanning is another leather processing method, relatively recent as the ancient leather industry goes. To achieve it the hide is filled with chromium compounds, and the result is a much softer, more pliable, and better wearing/lasting leather than that which has been vegetable-tanned. Most leather today, including most sheepskin, is chrome-tanned. Apparently it is easier for the tanner to color chrome-tanned leather, since this process is used exclusively when color is desired or applied. All of the shoe and moccasin leather you will use should be chrome-tanned and will be dyed in an enormous array of colors by the tanner.

Before dying, chrome-tanned leather is a grayish-greenish color, like chrome. If you make a small cut in a hide and look on the edge of the leather you can see a small line of gray; this is the chrome peeking through where the dye did not penetrate completely.

FINISH. Finish is the third factor in your selection of leather. The tanner can permeate "our" chrome-tanned leather with oil so that it has a rich, "leathery" feel. It can be finished in a tumbler that softens it further. Moccasin cowhide (our leather) does not have any synthetic finish on it, but is left with the pores open and soft. While this gets dirtier faster, it is magnificent to work with and highly desirable.

Sueding is a method of finishing the top grain. Here the hide is sanded or buffed to a velvety appearance. Our moccasin cow will have one side that is the top grain, smooth and sometimes velvety, and the other side will be very fuzzy, like suede, for reasons I described earlier in this chapter. I will refer to the reverse side as the suede side, although it is not technically suede. Very technically and traditionally speaking, suede was the back of the sheepskin, the side that doesn't have the wool. However, since cowhide tanning achievements have become so advanced, the technical definitions are very hazy these days. In making your shoes or moccasins, it does not make any difference which side you elect to use on the outside or inside, although

I feel the grain side holds up better because it can be waxed or oiled or polished or even dyed if necessary.

Some chrome-tanned leathers are finished on the top grain side with paint. These painted leathers are gray on the reverse side, since the hide was actually sprayed with paint rather than being dipped in a vat and permanently dyed. I never use this painted stuff. It looks like plastic and is much too stiff and unworkable.

MOCCASIN AND SHOE LEATHER. I keep referring to "our" kind of leather. This is because for years it has been relatively unpopular, somewhat difficult to find, and virtually nameless. It seems to be coming into its own these days, but for many years we had no name by which to call it and had only our hands to tell us if this was what we wanted. Today suppliers seem to be calling it moccasin cowhide, moc-cow, or bag leather. Whatever they call it, it is about 4–6 ounces, chrome-tanned, and dyed whatever color you want (or can find); it feels soft, smooth, and like something you'll enjoy having next to your foot.

I keep referring to selecting your leather. Whenever it is possible, do go personally to select the leather, rather than buying from mail-order sources. Cows are living animals. As such they get branded, roam pastures, and get cut on fences, get bitten by ticks, and gain weight rapidly before the slaughter. All of these incidents in their lives show up on the hide when it comes to you. They show up in the form of brands, stretch marks, holes in the leather, and scratches. Therefore, if you can personally select your hide, you can choose one that has the fewest imperfections.

Garment-weight leather is also smooth, soft,

chrome-tanned, and feels super. However, it is not heavy enough by itself for substantial, durable, well-shaped shoes or moccasins and will not hold up under the heavy pressure of a foot unless it is strongly reinforced with other materials such as cardboard. Deerskin is likewise too soft and very stretchy. If you get stuck and can't find moc-cow or bag leather, you can get garment weight and plan to use two thicknesses glued together for shoes or moccasins. This alternative will work well, but is an expensive way to go.

Whenever possible have a sample of the leather you want when you go to shop. Mail-order places will send samples on request. Salesmen frequently don't have time to help you, and when they do they often don't understand what you want. You are on your own. Here are some tests to help you in your selection.

Test 1. Manipulate the sides of the hide. Does the leather stretch easily? If it stretches, it will also compress and you will be able to work large amounts of leather into smaller amounts of space as when you gather the moccasin toe or mold the shoes. I count heavily on this stretch factor.

Test 2. Wad a small section in your hand. Does it fold close together with one crease in the fabric hitting the other, just as if you could wring it out? An unsuitable hide will fold with space between the folds because it is too stiff to squish together.

Test 3. A good-for-shoes hide will be very floppy. Roll it up and throw it over your shoulder. It should sag and flop and touch your back. By contrast, a latigo hide will rest on your shoulder like the old proverbial chip.

Finally. Will it feel good on your foot? Does it feel good and soft on your hand? Can you almost achieve a glove fit without even sewing it? Or does it bend awkwardly so that it sticks up in spots? Remember: trust yourself. If it feels good, it is.

A small word of discouragement. I personally hate to buy leather. It has become a highly frustrating, emotional ordeal in recent years. The price is up over 200 percent since 1970 with no end in sight, and the supply is very short. The supply of beef going to market is decreasing, while the demand, particularly from foreign countries, is very heavy. This translates to mean that fewer and fewer hides trickle down to our retail, little-person level. We get the rejected leather manufacturers can't use. There is a fair-sized list of suppliers in the back of the book, by no means complete, but you might still have to look and hunt to find good quality. Persist. Shoes will only be going up in price, and the shoes you create for yourself will be that much more valuable to you because they are well made and will last. When you do find what you want, may I recommend that you do what the woman suggested and "get it while you can—it may not be there tomorrow."

Sheepskin

The skin of the sheep with the wool still attached is called a sheepskin, although it is sometimes termed a shearling, sheepswool, or lambswool. Whatever sheepskins are called they are from small animals, the full hide being an average of only 7 to 9 feet and selling for . . . whatever they happen to be selling for that day. Everyone covets a pair of sheepskin moccasins, the only footwear for which you will be able to use sheepskin. It is the warmest, best natural insulation known, warm even when wet; it absorbs moisture and perspiration and feels great. A sheepskin is generally so pretty and looks so soft and warm one is reluctant to cut into it and ruin it.

Lots of people coming to me to choose a leather look at a plain sheepskin with the wool on one side and the skin on the other and think that I have somehow managed to glue these thousands of little hairs to the skin. This is the way sheepskin comes. The animal has an outer covering of woolly hairs that grow out of the skin. When the skin is removed from the body the wool is still attached to it. The wool may not be as long as it was on the living animal, but the original hairs are still on the skin. When you use sheepskin the wool is next to your foot and the skin side is the outside of the moccasin.

Tanneries have so many methods of tanning the sheepskin that it would be difficult to say what is a natural color. Sheepskins are generally bleached so that the wool side is white or yellowish and the skin side is a light gray. However, now that sheepskin coats are so popular, garment-weight skins are tanned so that the outside is any color the manufacturer wants or has ordered.

The wool of a sheepskin can be sheared or cut to various lengths, depending on the intended use. The full length is about 2 to 4 inches and is frequently left as is for rugs. A length of ½ inch or ¾ inch is ideal for moccasins, and a coat length is about ⅜ inch.

Generally the variation in quality of individual sheepskins is not as great as with cowhide. If you like the look of it, it is probably fine. The skin of a

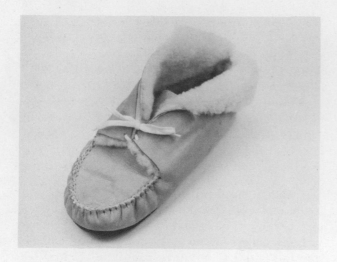

The skins are full of holes—big holes caused by gunshot wounds, by the animal's being dragged along the ground, and by poor skinning on the part of the hunter. You have to examine every hide carefully to make sure you have room to work around these holes and not have too much waste. These skins are also very expensive, but worth it for truly nice shoes or moccasins.

Buffalo is also a fine, heavy but soft leather although rather difficult to find. Other leathers, such as pigskin, goatskin, and calf, are not that wonderful to work with, they are rarely available in much quantity, and really not suitable for shoes or moccasins.

WORKING WITH LEATHER

Examining the Hide

Because leather is natural, you cannot treat it like a piece of cloth that is consistent and uniform throughout. Leather varies from hide to hide and within the hide. You will have to examine your hide or piece of leather before you begin, not just plop it down and start cutting. Frequently the tanner's blade slips in splitting the hide and there is a very weak, thin spot lurking within the best portions. You've got to look and feel for these weak areas and avoid them when you lay out your pattern and use the leather.

Leather is expensive. You can use every inch of it and you should plan to do so. Work from the edges toward the middle. You don't want to lay out a boot top, for example, that juts into the middle of the hide and divides it into two portions neither of which is large enough to accommodate a moccasin bottom or a shoe upper. Your pattern pieces are large, and you've got to plan things to allow for future projects.

Leather comes from an animal's body, and the quality varies in the same way meat from an animal's body varies in quality. The best portions of the cowhide correspond to the best pieces of the beef. The sirloin sections are along the back; the hamburger or not so perfect sections are around the animal's legs and at the extreme ends of the head and tail.

Stretch is a huge factor in leatherwork. Sometimes it works to your advantage. For example, if a boot top is cut too short, you can pull and yank on it until it stretches to the desired length, an extra ½ inch at least. This stretch can work against you, too. The shoe that fits perfectly today may be too big tomorrow. Therefore you try to look at and feel

sheepskin is very fragile and won't withstand much abuse. If your moccasins are to be anything more than house slippers, you should plan to cover the skin with another layer of leather. Consequently you will hide the skin portion of the sheepskin and are principally interested in the quality of the wool side. The skins are generally graded by the quality of the skin side, and you therefore can get the cheaper grades.

Some sheepskin is tanned specifically to be washed in warm water and dried in a hot dryer with no ill effects. This process was developed for hospitals, where the skins are placed under patients to prevent bedsores. You might want to get one of these specially treated skins if you want to wash your moccasins—they do get dirty. I have washed mine (which are made of regular sheepskin) in the cold water cycle of the washing machine and thrown them in the dryer—as I have also washed leather moccasins—with no noticeable effects, but I'm not sure the tanners would recommend this method. I wouldn't do it on a weekly basis, but if you get to the point of either throwing them out or washing them, wash them.

Other Leathers

Cowhide and sheepskin are the two most common, available leathers. Deerskin and elkskin are also fairly available, very popular, and wonderful to work with. Both are extremely soft and supple, therefore very stretchy. Generally they are extremely thin, and they should be used in two thicknesses or in combination with cowhide. The item should be thoroughly stressed and reinforced to prevent stretch and tear, since these skins are not as strong as cowhide.

your leather to determine which portions of the hide are stretchy. Generally around the leg portions is stretchy; it looks nice but will pull out of shape much too rapidly. This section is ideal for the lining next to your foot where it won't be pulled in many directions or bag and sag. Many parts of the hide are much stiffer than others, or tough. Notice these and plan to avoid using them for anything that you will be gathering or molding or will be next to your foot and might rub.

Some parts of the hide are aesthetically ugly. They might have tick or scratch or stretch marks. Fine, you just have to plan to work around these marks. They will show on a shoe upper but will not show up anywhere on a moccasin except the tongue piece. So you may plan to use these parts for your moccasins. Or you can turn the hide over and inspect the suede side under these marks. It might be very even and pretty and can easily be used as a moccasin boot top or for reinforcement pieces. You can mix the parts so that some are suede and some are grain and everyone thinks you are very creative when actually all you may be doing is efficiently utilizing what you have to its best advantage.

You'll love working with leather. It is the perfect substance for shoes because it breathes, is highly flexible and malleable, durable and pretty. It feels good. If you've ever worked with fabric, you'll find you won't have many of the annoying and time-consuming tasks that you have with cloth. There is no particular bias or direction of grain to be concerned with. You can put any pattern piece down anywhere you select on the hide in any direction and have it work as well as any other direction. You can and should fit all your pattern pieces closely together so there is no wasted material. You don't have to worry about matching plaids or prints or even grain. Leather will not fray; you don't need pinking shears or extra binding or folded seams. The extra pieces of leather may be nice from a finishing point of view, or for reinforcement, but they are not essential for making the shoe wear. They can be put on the outside of the item as decoration instead of hidden inside.

Leather does have drawbacks. It is so much thicker and bulkier than fabric that you should avoid seams whenever possible; they will show, and you can't iron them down and make them disappear or fix bad fits with a tuck here or a dart there. Everything must be preplanned exactly.

And don't forget that leather is not particularly washable. If you want your items to end up looking nice, keep your hands clean, spread the hide out where the dog and children can't wander all over it, and don't use newspaper for your paper patterns. It can't be basted, as material can. Once you have put glue on the edges, the glue line will show and change the color of that area. Once you have sewn it, the stitch holes are in and visible. Although you can take the item apart and redo it, you may have to live with little holes you'd rather weren't there.

For each piece of leather that goes into the shoe or moccasin you will make a pattern. In transferring your pattern to the leather you have to use a fine-lined pen to make a mark, or a scratch awl, needle, or sharp pointed object to mark or score it. You cannot pin the pattern in place and absolutely cannot hold it in place and cut around it. The pattern pieces are designed to be exact and must be cut exactly. The finer the pen line you use, the less these marks will show on the finished item. These marks won't be hidden in a seam or tucked away as with fabric. When you transfer your pattern to leather, hold it down and very carefully draw around the pattern, following each line. Don't use a crayon or felt-tipped pen or anything with a thick line. When you cut the leather you will want to follow the line exactly, and it's more difficult with a thick line.

You will have to spend a lot of time cutting out your leather. In order to do a good job it takes time. These cuts will be visible or matched to another piece, and the only way you can be sure they will be right is to make sure you have an exact replica of your pattern. If my directions say cut it out, I don't mean zip-presto chomp them out the fastest way you can. I mean take time and care and patience and do the cutting so that the lines are smooth and even. Whether you cut with shears or a knife, it must be done neatly. Also take particular care to cut your paper patterns out so that they are absolutely clean and smooth. You certainly can't get a good replica of the pattern on leather if you're following hacked-out paper patterns. Just because the point isn't made repeatedly doesn't mean forget it: always cut everything out carefully.

Latigo and heavier leathers are harder to cut than softer leathers; they take more time and physical energy. The soft leathers can be stretchy, and your result can be thrown way off if you are not careful.

Soling

Soling is the other very important part of the shoe, and your selection in types of soling these days is enormous. Shoes now are described by their purpose, rather than their style as they used to be, and generally the purpose is designated by the type of soling used rather than the design of the upper. The popular notion that just because shoes are handmade you are stuck with leather soling is no longer true. If you are really into some activity —jogging, tennis, golf, boating, hiking, bowling, etc., etc.—you are now in a position to make any or all of these shoes for yourself. Or if you just want a good all-around shoe that will do for most sports and activities, you can make that as well. The choice is entirely yours and generally no more involved than selecting the right soling and popping it on the shoe. It really is lots of fun.

The place to buy soling is a shoe findings store. These stores are joys to explore, and whole new worlds open to you in them because nearly any kind of soling is available—many you have never seen or thought of—and your mind spins with the possibilities. The very nicest thing about buying soling is that it is dependable and reliable. After the anxious and frustrating trips to the leather suppliers your trips to the shoe findings store can be quiet, pleasant events. Soling is always available in the same sizes, the same colors, the same thicknesses, and the prices rarely fluctuate. Once you have worked with one type of soling you will know how it behaves and it will always behave the same way. This is a very nice change of pace from the constant fluctuation in quality, quantity, and price of leather.

Soling materials fall into two classifications: leather and rubber or synthetic. To help you get a comparative idea of the various solings, look at the

chart listing the important qualities. This is certainly not a complete list, and it is heavily prejudiced by our use of the different materials over the years. I certainly don't expect you to try them all immediately, if ever. There are a dozen or more types and you might be interested in experimenting at some time. I'll run over these characteristics on the chart and in the process discuss soling.

QUALITIES TO CONSIDER

THICKNESS. Soling is measured and sold by the "iron." This is an antique English system of measurement with 48 irons to the inch. Thus, if you decide you want to use a sole about ¼ inch thick, you ask for 12-iron soling, if you want ½-inch thickness, it is 24 iron, and so on. Generally the rubber solings are standardized in increments of 3 irons: 6 iron, 9 iron, 12, 15, 18, 21, and 24 are the popular thicknesses, and 36 iron is about the thickest I have seen. Leather soling is natural and can measure out to any thickness.

HOW SOLD. Bends, sheets, or blanks.

Bends. Leather soling can be sold by the bend, a rectangle of leather cut from the back of the cowhide. It measures approximately 50 by 25 inches and will make soles for at least twenty pairs of shoes or sandals. Bends are sold in many thicknesses, generally running between 9 and 12 iron, and they are sold by the pound, since a bend of 11/12 iron will weigh more than one of 9/10 iron. As with all leather, a bend is not uniformly thick throughout and is thus referred to in a general range of thicknesses. Because a bend is so big, is extremely heavy to move around and work with, and you are stuck with material for twenty pairs of shoes, it is not something you want to get the first time out.

Sheets. Rubber solings are sold in sheets, not nearly as large as a bend. They measure around 36 by 18 or 25 inches depending on type and manufacturer. A standard sheet of crepe will yield about six pairs of soles.

Blanks. Much soling, including some leather, is sold in pairs. Leather is sold this way so that quality and iron can be matched. Rubber is sold this way for convenience, so you don't have to stock up on expensive types, or some soles such as Vibram are molded to a particular shape and matched. When you buy these, don't just get the size you wear; measure your pattern for length and width and get whatever size fits your pattern. These blanks are definitely the cheaper way to go if you want to experiment with a certain type of soling or are not booked solid with orders. The same is true with leather because although blanks are more expensive per pair than bends, you get what you pay for and you aren't stuck with a lot of extra you won't use for months. Bends sold at leather supply houses are inconsistent in thickness, being right off the hide, and you frequently run into the problem of having one shoe slightly thicker than the other or thicker at the heel than the toe.

COLOR. Obvious.

TEXTURE. Most of the solings have some sort of pattern or texture on the bottom to provide added grip. Any soling with texture is an improvement over slick leather soling, although I haven't found one yet that will grab on ice.

WEARABILITY. This is always important to your customer and always difficult to assess, since everyone walks different distances on different substances.

Solings	Thickness (irons)	How Sold (sheets, bends, blanks)	Color	Texture (outside)	Wearability	Workability	Flexibility	Use	Comments
Vegetable-, oak-, or bark-tanned leather	8–15	bends, blanks	flesh pink	smooth (slippery)	average	difficult	poor—stiff	shoes, sandals	Hard to cut. Can be wetted and molded. Burnishes beautifully.
Chrome-tanned leather	6–12	bends	grayish	smooth	excellent	difficult	bends easily	all	The better leather soling.
Crepe	12–24	sheets (36 × 50), blanks	black, white, red, brown, gray	smooth	average	easy	excellent	shoes, sandals, heavy moccasins	Superior all-round soling for shoes and sandals.
Squeegee (boat) crepe	21	sheets (36 × 24)	white	lined	below average	easy	excellent	all	
Tennis shoe crepe	12	sheets (36 × 24)	white	indented	below average	easy	excellent	all	
Natural (plantation) gum rubber	18	sheets (24 × 36), blanks	white, cream	bumpy	poor	very difficult	bends	shoes, sandals	Very difficult to work with. Dissolves in oil or gas.
Imitation (gristle) gum rubber	9	sheets (24 × 36)	cream	bumpy	average	easy	excellent	all	Nice stuff.
Galosh or dance rubber	3	sheets (12 × 24)	black, brown	small cross-lines	average	easy	superior	moccasins	Superior all-round moccasin soling. Inside must be sanded before gluing.
Vibram	24	blanks	black	lugs (grips)	excellent	very difficult	stiff	shoes, sandals	Should probably be used only for hiking boots.
Ripple	15 & 24	blanks	black, brown	ripples (grips)	excellent	hard	bends	shoes, sandals, heavy moccasins	Good walking soling.
Ribbed	6	sheets (24 × 36)	cream	ribs (grips)	average	easy	excellent	moccasins, light shoes	
Neolite	12	sheets (24 × 36), blanks	brown	smooth (slippery)	excellent	very difficult	stiff	shoes, sandals	Avoid.

Most of the solings wear fairly well. Thickness is not necessarily an indication of wearability. I've stopped trying to make things last forever. Make them comfortable and right for you. After all, you are making the shoe and can easily resole it for pennies.

WORKABILITY.   How easy or difficult is it to cut, to glue onto the shoe, and how readily can it be sanded away? This quality is important if you want to keep enjoying your work. If you're not muscular it isn't fun to hack and saw at leather soling just to cut out the general shape; it isn't fun to throw all your strength behind a hammer just to get something to stick together; and it definitely isn't fun to stand at the sander for hours inhaling powdered rubber, wiping it out of your eyes, and covering everything around you with dust. So I definitely lean toward the easy-to-work-withs.

FLEXIBILITY.   How easily does it bend? This is important to you not only in wearing the shoe but in selecting the right soling for a particular kind of footwear. Flexibility is directly related to the weight of a product and to the density. It is not necessarily related to the thickness, since many products are filled with air.

USE.   Any soling can be used on any footwear, if it is properly designed. If you purposely design a heavy-duty working moccasin to withstand the stress and pull of ripple soling, you can use it, but you can't just slap it on an ordinary moccasin and expect it to stay.

TYPES OF SOLING

Leather

As with regular leather, there are at least two kinds of leather solings: vegetable-, oak-, or bark-tanned and chrome-tanned, as well as several oily combination types. All are thick and heavy, and few people recognize them as being the hide of an animal.

VEGETABLE-TANNED LEATHER.   The most frequently used leather soling is the vegetable-tanned, which has a pink look to it, is very smooth and shiny on the grain side, is stiff and gets stiffer after you've walked through water, and is very heavy and very difficult to work with and cut. Shoe findings stores sell this leather in blanks which have been graded according to quality—prime through poor—and thickness. It is sometimes available in 3-iron thickness, called ladies' soling, which is nice if what you want to make is a very lightweight slippery shoe. Vegetable-tanned leather is extremely slippery, which makes it great for dancing shoes, but you take your chances anywhere else. Always put on a thin rubber heel, if you use leather soling, to prevent broken backs.

A plus for this soling is that it can be shined to a magnificent gloss and luster and the edge of the shoe looks incredibly finished and professional. It is the best soling to use if you plan to nail because the stiffness and density of this leather makes placing the nails easy and holds them well.

CHROME-TANNED LEATHER.   This soling is very light and flexible in comparison to bark-tanned; it is relatively nonslip and far more durable. All in all a quality soling, but it isn't a dream to work with either. It has a grayish cast to it, and the edges are very hard to polish and always seem to look ragged and shaggy no matter what you do. Of the two types of leather, though, it is the better quality.

Artificial Soles

Personally, I rarely use leather soling anymore. People rarely request it, and it fluctuates in price and availability like all leather. It is hard to work with and doesn't offer much excitement or variety.

CREPE.   This is my all-round choice for shoes and sandals. It is highly flexible and workable, is completely waterproof, has great cushioning for walking or standing, comes in a wide variety of thicknesses and colors, and isn't terribly expensive. Crepe is the only soling that has no specific inside or outside texture, and it still gives good traction. This two-sidedness is a decided advantage, since it means you can glue several layers together to make a high wedge or use it as heeling. It is very lightweight and probably doesn't wear quite as well as leather, but you can use a layer of it to give the shoe height and shock absorbency and then glue on a final layer of thin gristle soling or something thin but dense which will take the wear and tear of concrete better.

There are at least five thicknesses available, from 12 iron to 24 iron. I would suggest you start your shoemaking with a sheet of 18- or 21-iron crepe. For some reason the white crepe is much heavier and denser then the black; thus a 21-iron white will be less flexible then a 21-iron black.

Athletic solings. Squeegee boat soling, tennis shoe soling, and other athletic solings are all forms of crepe. The squeegee has small cuts in the bottom which are supposed to add to the grip on a wet deck, and the tennis shoe has ⅛-inch indentations that are supposed to give added traction without added weight.

Gum rubber crepe. Plantation, natural, and Malaysian crepe rubber are made with real rubber, are white or cream, and look like dried rubber cement. Very common on many ready-made shoes. This natural crepe does not wear nearly as well as it looks like it will and has one bad disadvantage, aside from being impossible to work with. The sole dissolves in gas and oil or starts dissolving on contact with it and becomes sticky and squeaky on floors.

GRISTLE. There is an imitation "natural" gum rubber, called gristle, which works beautifully in all ways. It is thin but dense, so it wears well, and it gives good traction. It starts in a 9-iron thickness and is super for sheepskin moccasins with a light midsole, children's footwear, and even lightweight shoes.

GALOSH OR DANCE RUBBER. Called by either name, this is perfect for maintaining the traditional wraparound soft fit of a moccasin without sacrificing durability. It may be unauthentic to put a rubber sole on a moccasin, but it saves the moccasin from certain ruin without it. The sole, only 3 iron or ⅙ inch thick, is crisscrossed with small cuts or indentations that give very good traction, protect your feet from pebbles and rocks, and wear incredibly well; for at least a year of everyday normal use. I definitely recommend that you start your moccasin work

with this soling. Because of its extreme thinness—it is the thinnest soling made—you can just glue it to the bottom of the moccasin and it will stick. However, if you want it to stay on, you must sand the inner side of the soling thoroughly, until every bit of the shiny surface is gone.

VIBRAM AND RIPPLE SOLING. There are many heavy solings sold in blanks designed for specific uses. Vibram and Ripple are the most popular in this category. Both these soles are very thick, very durable, and heavy.

Vibram was originally designed for rock climbing and has heavy, deep ½-inch lugs (or thick cubes) on the bottom which can be jammed into small crevasses in the rock. Vibram is so heavy that it must be used with an equally heavy upper to withstand the strain, and the result is generally a very stiff, inflexible shoe quite unsuitable for street use. It picks up mud and small pebbles easily.

Vibram comes in blanks with or without the heel attached and is difficult to work with. The true Vibram brand has an unattached heel, which has to be nailed on, and therefore you have to use a leather sole as a midsole. To be safe you should nail on the toe section as well, because it has a strong inclination to peel away. Shoe repairers charge a high price for Vibram soles with good reason. They are expensive to buy and a bear to work with. They wear like iron and feel the same way. They do supposedly give good snow traction.

Ripple soles were designed by a shoe specialist to go on a good flexible shoe that has lots of bounce as you walk. It is thick, but the ripples—more or less like waves—are very deep and run across the foot so they bend and flex when the foot does. They are super for standing all day, give good traction, and don't seem to pick up mud and debris like Vibram. Ripple soles come in two weights or thicknesses, the bantamweight being for lighter shoes. Ripple soles also come with an optional wedge which gives much better support than a heel and is much easier to attach. Ripple, like Vibram, will also wear like iron but feels great.

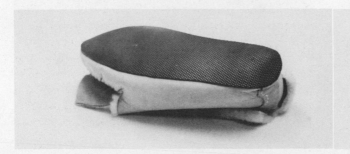

Padding

I put padding in every shoe, sandal, or moccasin that I make and strongly recommend that you plan to use it. All of the finest footwear uses and advertises a soft cushioned inner sole—what I so unceremoniously call padding. The Indians and Colonials were aware of its advantages and stuffed their shoes and moccasins with hay or grass or moss, especially in winter to add warmth. I like to think that foam rubber is an improvement on moss, but it uses the same principle. It adds tremendous comfort to the shoe, plus insulation so that there is more between you and the ground.

One fabulous advantage of using padding is that it does pack down. Once it has, it conforms exactly to the bottom of your foot, and thus it completely eliminates the need to do any elaborate moldings of the foot bottom or make lasts or foot castings. Generally speaking, the way it conforms also eliminates the need for arch supports.

Although there are many types of open- and closed-celled rubbers, ordinary foam rubber seems to be about the best available. The shoe findings stores sell a padding they call orthopedic foam which works well but costs a fortune and isn't worth it. Carpet padding breaks down rapidly, sources are unreliable, and qualities and thicknesses vary widely.

The best foam rubber is the densest, heaviest weight of ordinary foam rubber in 1-inch thickness. Generally you can get it in upholstery supply stores in flat sheets a yard square or you can order it through the large catalog stores. It is very inexpensive. If you cannot locate the heavy-density kind, use a lighter density in a layer even thicker than an inch, up to 2 inches. It will easily compact and be extremely comfortable.

All my directions for making footwear are based on the assumption that you will be using this padding and that it will be 1 to 2 inches thick. It doesn't make too much difference what thickness you use in the shoes and sandals—as far as fit—but it is critical in making moccasins. The fit of your moccasins might be off if you use less thickness or a lighter density.

The procedure for making the pattern and cutting the padding is the same for all the footwear, so I'll explain it once.

To determine the size of the padding, use the sole pattern (see individual chapters) of the item you are making. Make a tracing of the sole pattern and measure in from the edges of this tracing ⅜ inch all the way around. Cut out the smaller sole pattern. This is the padding pattern.

Lay the pattern on your foam rubber and trace around it with a felt pen. (A felt pen is about the only thing that will make a mark on foam rubber.) Now cut the padding out. Couldn't be simpler.

Foam rubber is sort of funny to cut. You have to chomp your way around with the shears. But a smooth, even cut isn't important, since the foam rubber will never be seen. It will be sandwiched between a sole or midsole and an inner lining or topsole, two pieces of leather that will be glued together.

The only important thing to remember is that you have to be able to lay that padding over the sole, moccasin bottom, or whatever and see a margin or rim of leather all the way around it. If you can't see about a ¼-inch rim you won't be able to glue the pieces together, or if you manage to they won't stay glued. So trim the foam until you have that margin.

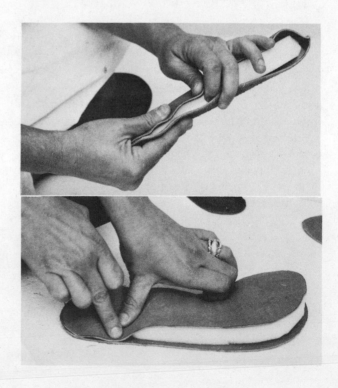

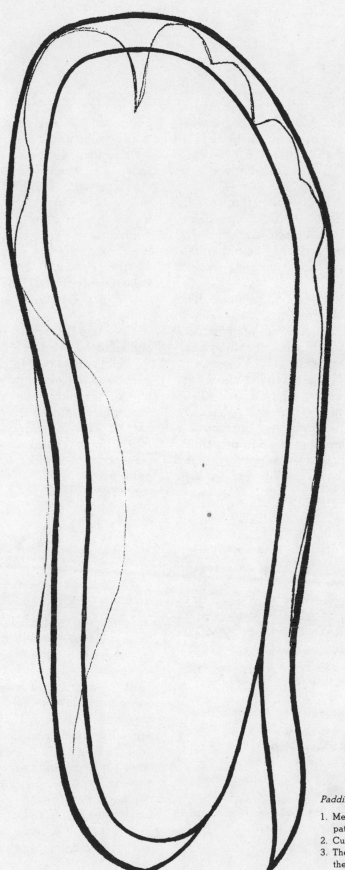

Padding Pattern

1. Measure in from the edge of the sole pattern line ⅜"
2. Cut away the excess.
3. The small pattern is now the padding pattern.

Tools

Shoemaking is just about the least expensive and most practical hobby, craft, or trade that I know about. You can get an exhilarated, I've-beat-the-system feeling when you realize what you can accomplish with a small bag of hand tools, a few materials, two good hands, and a functioning mind. You will need very few tools—knife, shears, hammer, punch, stitcher, needle, thread, and glue—in order to make shoes. You probably have several already, and all of them are extremely useful around the house.

Good tools are dear friends to a craftsperson. But like dear friends, you only need a few very good ones, not a large assemblage of acquaintances. Because salesmen are in the business of selling and beginning craftspeople are easy prey, I also mention in passing a few tools that you don't need, but that salesmen and sales catalogs say you cannot live without. If I don't mention a tool, it isn't because I don't know about it (leather tools have been essentially the same for two hundred years) but simply that for one reason or another—poor quality, high cost, bad design, and so on—I think you can easily live without it. I've tried to list things that you can buy locally, at hardware stores and such. I think it is easier and you'll have more selection.

Shoe findings stores specialize in supplies for shoe repair shops. I prefer to buy from them rather than from leather supply houses which specialize in selling to hobbyists and "leatherworkers." It may be my cynical nature, but I just feel that the shoe findings stores, generally located in some grubby, low-rent district, are set up to help supply you with what you *need,* rather than sell you things that seem to be terribly crafty. Check your local Yellow Pages under "Shoe Findings"; every large city has such a place.

One other thing—safety. Your tools are designed and selected to cut through heavy leather and soling and to do it fast. Watch your fingers. While they aren't number one on the dangerous hobby list—like woodworking—shoemaking and leatherwork are right up there with their sharp knives, heavy hammers, shears, and such. I certainly don't want to sound like your mother, but do be careful, have respect for your tools, don't buy any that are stupidly designed, and don't continue to use them if you don't feel comfortable with them.

stitching awl
with needle in place

GLUE

In leatherwork, your glue just might be the most essential "tool" in your shop. The modern-day contact cements are the one thing that have changed the trade of shoemaking in the past hundred years. Most commercial shoes are held together in part or entirely by these glues. As any shoe buyer knows, they are darn good, but for durability they can't replace sewing or nailing.

Barge Contact Cement is so superior to any of the other glues on the market that there is no second choice. To use, apply the glue to *both* surfaces of the leathers to be joined, wait for them to become tacky to the touch, and put them together. Once you have put them together it is almost impossible to separate them, and if you are able to separate them you will have to pull the leather, soling, or whatever

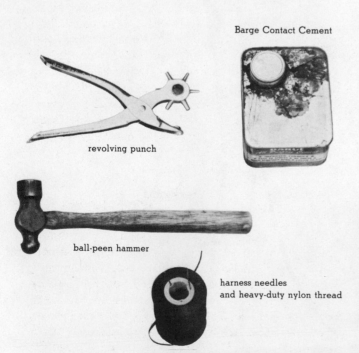

Barge Contact Cement

revolving punch

ball-peen hammer

harness needles
and heavy-duty nylon thread

so that it stretches and tears and loses its shape. So be careful and make it right the first time.

This cement takes quite a while to become tacky or dry, at least 10 or 20 minutes, depending on the weather, the side of the leather being glued, and other factors. This is its major disadvantage and is frustrating because you can't proceed until the pieces are together. Be patient and don't rush it. Don't try to take a shortcut by buying one of the quick-drying cements; they simply don't have Barge's holding power: the whole purpose of glue to begin with. Many shoe findings stores have a "house" glue they claim is just as good as Barge only much cheaper. Don't get it—Barge is one product that stands alone. When you glue on a sole, the glue is the only thing holding it on. People simply don't enjoy having their soles fall off; for some silly reason it annoys them.

The glue is sold in 4-ounce "student" cans, quart cans, and gallons. You'll be using a lot of it, so start with the quart can. It dries up quickly if you leave the top unscrewed while you are working. If it dries up too much, get some thinner for it. Thinner is also handy for removing glue from your clothes and hands after you've been working and for dissolving it when you are trying to remove old soling.

Do follow the directions on the can. When they say use it only in a well-ventilated room they mean a well-ventilated room, because the glue contains toluene, which ruins brain cells.

As you use it, spread it on smoothly and evenly. Don't glob it on, but don't be miserly either. The "suede" side of leather absorbs glue more than the leather (grain) side, so you'll have to apply it a bit more heavily on the suede side. I realize it sounds wrong to say let the glue dry before using it, but that is the way contact cement works—it makes contact with itself and sticks together.

Very oily leathers—latigo particularly and some of the moccasin cowhides—do not take glue at all well. We've done everything to make them take it, and almost nothing works. Sometimes it helps to apply a primer coat of glue and let it dry before applying a final coat.

CUTTING TOOLS

utility knife

small curved knife

Knives

Shoes simply cannot be made without a very good, very sharp knife. In my years of shoemaking and experimentation I've been as seduced by salesmen as any other novice and have ended up with a fascinating collection of oddly shaped knives that I never use. I cannot recommend a single knife that is sold by the supply houses for shoemaking.

First, you need an ordinary hardware-brand utility knife. This knife screws together and has replaceable blades. There are many shapes and sizes; get the one that feels the best in your hand, not the cheapest one. The blades cost, but they are always razor sharp and will cut anything easily, even the thickest soling. Also, the blades can either be put away inside the handle or be retracted, a safety measure I think essential.

Second, I constantly use a little beauty we got in a quality hardware store. It was originally designed to be a vegetable paring knife. It resembles traditional leatherworking knives in that it has the same small curve, but without the lethal hook traditional leatherworking knives have on the end. A curved knife is necessary if you are to cut away excess soling from the curves of the shoe. This little knife is a Henckels, made in Germany, and it cost, at the time we bought it, somewhere around $5—expensive but well worth it. It is made of high-quality tempered steel, and even a dullard like me can sharpen it. Notice the handle—quality knives have the blade extending into the handle and riveted all the way through both sides of the wood and through the blade. This means that the blade will not fall out and will not wiggle as you are cutting. Look for such a knife in a good cutlery store.

There is an old adage that a dull knife is unsafe. It's true. A dull knife does not make a smooth, deep, clean cut. You have to hack and saw, you get angry, and you vent all your hostility on the piece of soling, completely forgetting that the knife is a lethal weapon. You forget that your fingers are still easy to cut compared to soling. Do keep your knife sharp; it is well worth it to you. If you can't sharpen it, don't use it dull. If you aren't comfortable using a knife and don't feel you have complete control over it, don't use it.

Shears

You'll be doing a lot of cutting, and you should have a very good pair of shears. They are expensive, but on the bright side, they last. Good-quality shears are made of strong forged steel and can be sharpened. Mine are Wiss, about the best name in scissors or shears. They have 8-inch blades and can be purchased, around town, at upholstery supply stores. My second pair, bent shears, have a handle designed to enable you to cut keeping the blade and handle on the table. It's definitely an asset. A very good knife sharpener (hard to find—ask your local barber whom he uses) can put a serrated edge on one of the blades which lets the shears grab and hold the leather so it doesn't slip as you cut. Good dressmaking shears, made for heavy cloth, also work well. Don't get those plastic-handled things they claim will cut anything: they won't. Also, don't get the belt and leather shears which are heavier, fatter, and shorter then ordinary shears and supposedly designed to cut the very heavy latigos. They don't, and they don't cut soft leathers at all.

Edger

The edger beveler bevels and cleans away excess leather from the edge of a piece of leather. It's a sandal tool used on straps after they've been stripped from the hide, and gives the strap a nice finished appearance. It's also useful for trimming away excess ragged edges from the topsole of a sandal or the top edge of a shoe after you've sanded it. Edgers come in several price ranges and sizes. For overall use, size 3 in the medium-priced group is good. They say you can sharpen this with wet-dry sandpaper, although I've had no success.

To use this tool, put the heel of the edger on the leather and shove it. No heavy pressure needed—try to get one continuous strip or thread of leather as you push it along.

Stripper

A stripper is variously called a stripper, draw gauge, or strap cutter. Its function is to cut an even, long strap or strip away from a hide. A necessity for sandals, it is of little value in making shoes or moccasins, since it can be used only with latigo or heavy leather. Soft leathers are too soft to strip.

There are several kinds. The cheapest one, the Strip-eze, costs about $2. It is made of wood and uses an ordinary single-edged razor blade for cutting. It's great for the money and for the amount you use it.

The most expensive, steel, hollow-handle type costs more than $20 and simply isn't worth the investment. Other, newer designs don't appear to me to be impressive, and I've never bought them. Get the inexpensive model.

The stripper can be set to any desired width; ¼ inch is about as thin as you can reliably cut. Be sure to check the markings on the stripper against a real ruler, because the stripper ruler is always inaccurate. Using the stripper is a matter of downward pressure with your left hand and arm holding the cut strap, and upward pressure with your right hand pulling the stripper.

This works only if you are drawing against one edge that is already straight and even. If you have a fresh latigo hide that does not have a ruler-straight side to it, you will have to create one before you can cut straps from it. Lay the hide out, with the back to you (because the back portion is practically straight to begin with). Take a yardstick and draw a straight line all the way down the side of the back, as close to the edge as possible, to create your straight edge. Then use a good sharp utility knife and cut along this line, cutting away the uneven excess. After that excess is eliminated you'll have a perfectly straight edge from which to cut away straps with the stripper.

edger

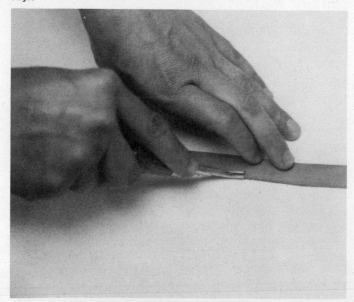

stripper

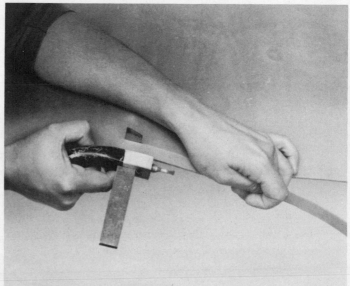

sole cutter

Sole Cutter

Not surprisingly, the sole cutter is designed to cut the foot shape out of heavy soling and is super to have if you get into a lot of work. It is extremely helpful in cutting out leather soles, which are so grim to do by hand. It operates in the same way a can opener does, cranked with the left hand and guided with the right. There are no electric parts to malfunction, so you are perfectly safe in getting a used one if you feel your work load demands it.

Cutting Board

By no means do you need an elaborate cutting and punching board; simply use an old board that you don't mind ruining, unless you feel that way about your dining-room table.

PUNCHING TOOLS

Revolving Punch

The most necessary item in the grand assortment of punching tools is the revolving punch. In one tool you have a small tube to punch the holes for sewing your moccasins, a large tube to punch the holes for laces when the moccasins are finished, and four other-sized holes in between.

The tubes press through the leather and hit a copper anvil or plate on the other side. This plate becomes indented with all the various-sized holes, and it doesn't take long until the punch is not making a clean cut, but a chewed and ragged one, if any. This has happened on my expensive punch as well as the cheap one. Use a scrap of leather as a backing piece behind or under the leather you are punching. This makes the original hole perfect and the scrap cut bad.

The expensive Osborn punch will last a lifetime, has replaceable tubes, but isn't worth the 300 percent jump in price over the cheap brands.

Osborn also makes single-hole punches which are very useful and comfortable to use if you find yourself making a lot of moccasins and punching a lot of small holes.

Slot Punch

The slot or oblong punch is used to punch slots in sandal topsoles so the straps can pass through them. It differs from the revolving punch not only in the shape and size of the hole it makes but in that you hammer on it to make the hole rather than squeezing handles. Naturally, slot punches come in sizes depending on the size hole you need for the straps. We have a ⅜-inch, a ½-inch, and a ⅝-inch one. Start with the ½-inch size as a good median.

Manufacturers recommend that you use the punch with a block of end-grain wood underneath. I have always used a piece of soling over the anvil, and it works out adequately. In any case, you must have something under the punch into which it can penetrate slightly after cutting through the leather. If you don't, the metal will fracture and the tool will be useless.

STITCHING TOOLS

Thread

If you want your finished products to hold together for years to come, you must use the best thread available. Waxed nylon thread is the very best. Linen and cotton are traditional, but they both rot. Many leather goods fall apart because the thread has rotted or torn the leather. Nylon does not rot, it is much stronger than cotton or linen, and it

slot punch

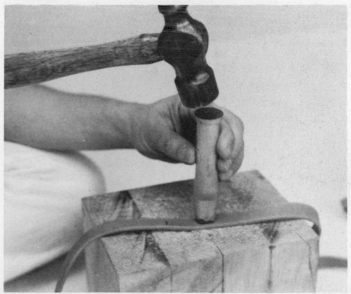

stretches and gives with the leather. The wax lets the thread slip through without resistance.

My thread is very heavy: seventeen strands of nylon interwoven. It will not break or split or tear, ever. It is superior to any other thread I have ever used or seen. Unfortunately, it is sold only by mail order (see Suppliers at end of book for manufacturers' catalog numbers). A second-choice thread, available at leather suppliers, is made by the Speedy Stitcher Company and is quite good and easier to get. The heavier the thread, the easier it is to work with and the longer it will last. Whatever you select, be certain it is waxed nylon.

Nylon thread does not knot well, and it can easily pull apart at a knot because of the wax. To make your knot frayless, singe the ends of the thread and the knot until it becomes one melted, lumpy ball with the ends fused together so they cannot come apart.

Stitching Awl

A stitching awl is a very strong, round steel needle inserted into a handle called an awl haft and screwed into place. It is especially designed to sew leather. Needle and awl haft are sold separately at shoe findings supply stores. The handles come in plastic or wood, plastic being the better choice, and both are nice and small and fit comfortably in the palm of your hand. The needle to buy is a Speedy Stitcher number 8, the strongest, longest, and straightest one made; curved ones are available, but you'll have no need for them.

This is the most basic of sewing machines. You'll use it whenever you want to sew two overlapping pieces of leather together. It takes some practice to develop the ability to sew evenly spaced, ruler-straight lines of stitches, and then more practice to gather speed. But there is plenty of opportunity to practice, since all your shoes are sewed with this tool and you use it to add all tops, reinforcement pieces, and decorative stitching. It sews anything heavy like car upholstery, canvas bags, etc., and is useful around the house.

There are several brands of ready-to-use stitchers on the market. Among them the Speedy Stitcher used to be the finest, but the quality of machining the threads of the screw parts is now so poor I have been forced to switch to and recommend the awl/needle combination. These ready-to-use stitchers, including the Speedy Stitcher, have a number of unnecessary features such as a place to store extra needles and a small spool on which to wind thread. This spool adds a lot of bulk to the tool, making it

thick in your hand, plus, on some designs, it is positioned between your hand and the needle with the result that you don't have the control over the needle you do with the awl haft. Of course, if you already have a stitcher, do use it, but all of the students who tried both designs preferred the awl as more comfortable and easier to use.

Operating this stitcher is simple once you understand it. Don't try to make it complex; it isn't. Like a sewing machine, you will have a top thread and a bobbin thread working together to create a strong lock stitch. If you use waxed nylon thread, this stitch will not come apart.

The needle is very finely made. The shaft, or bottom portion, is round. At the very tip or needle part, it has three sides, under which is the hole for the thread to go through. Two sides converge into a short groove, ½ inch long. The third side becomes a long groove or rounded depression in the needle which extends the full length of the needle.

Thread the needle going from the long grooved side to the short grooved side, and for the first stitch draw only about ½ inch of thread through the hole. Pass the threaded needle through the leather pieces you are sewing together from the top to the bottom. If you have any problem with the needle slipping in the handle when you sew through all those layers of material, tighten the chuck with pliers.

When you push the handle in, also twist the stitcher and the needle will slip in faster. Don't be afraid of the needle. Leather is tough and generally consistently tough, so the needle won't suddenly pop through and into your finger. I keep my finger directly under the needle to add pressure as I am pushing, and then when I feel it coming through, I quickly move my finger aside. Your finger might get nicked a bit, but nothing catastrophic.

On the side of the leather on which the needle has come out, the bottom, grab the piece of thread, hold on to it, and withdraw the needle back through the hole to the original side. This leaves the end of the thread on the side of the leather opposite your stitcher. This thread now operates the same way a bobbin does in a sewing machine. Pull the thread through the hole until the piece on the "bobbin" side of the leather is about double the distance you plan to sew. Don't cut the thread; leave it attached to the spool.

The second time you poke the needle through the leather, push it as far as it will go, then pull it back to about half the needle length. This will cause the thread to form a loop on the short-grooved side of the needle. Stick the end of the "bobbin" thread through this loop, withdraw the needle, and you have a stitch. Pull both sides of the thread tight and try to bury the knot between the two pieces of leather. Now just stitch along the same way until you have finished.

Stitch length is a matter of individual taste. The smaller the stitches, the prettier the stitching looks. Don't try to get them much smaller than 3/16 inch—it takes too much time.

On the top or stitcher side of the leather, always allow enough slack thread to cover the distance of the stitch plus *the entire length of the needle*. Here's why. As you thrust the needle through the leather it must go through the entire length of the needle. The thread must also. It must. If you haven't allowed enough thread to extend the length of the needle, the thread will have to come from somewhere, and the somewhere is the previous stitch. The result will be a gathered, too-tight stitching job, and quite frequently a bent or broken needle.

Don't disconnect the thread from the spool until the last stitch. To tie off the thread at the end of your sewing, before making the last stitch, cut the thread from the spool/stitcher side, leaving about 2 inches. Poke the needle through the leathers, take the thread out of the needle, and tie the two ends together in a square knot.

Harness Needle

The harness needle (Osborn number 00) is a 2-inch needle with a blunt end so that it will not catch on the leather as you sew. It is used when you cannot use your stitcher and involves prepunching holes (the smallest on your revolving punch) and then, with the needle, sewing or lacing the leather together. You will use this method to butt two pieces of leather together—edge to edge, not overlapping —as with the heel of both the moccasin and the shoe, and to sew the toe of the moccasin. Generally this method uses a simple cross-stitch, and it can also be used for spots where you want decorative stitching.

MEASURING TOOLS

In making my transition to craftsperson, relearning to use and read the ruler was my most difficult adjustment. It is measure, measure, measure all the time. If you are like I was, you haven't seriously looked at a ruler and all those little marks since you were in fifth grade. Certainly the last thing I want to do is insult you now, but just in case it has slipped your mind, I'll run over them. If you don't need a refresher, skip this.

We all know about feet and yards, but most of us ignore the division marks within the inch that are so critical in craftwork.

A standard, cheap plastic ruler is set up with 12 inches on one side and the metric scale on the other. Since few tools, much less our minds, are set up metrically, just ignore that side.

An inch is commonly spoken of as being divided into eight parts, although on most rulers those eight parts are again divided and the inch becomes sixteen parts. Notice that the division marks are of varying lengths. The longest lines show the inch divisions. The next longest divide the inch into half-inches. Then two lines divide the half-inches into quarter-inches. Each quarter is divided by a shorter line which marks the eighths, and eighths are finally divided again into sixteenths of an inch.

Nothing confusing about it, just divisions. If I say measure out a line 3/8 inch, just remember that 3/8 is 1/4 plus 1/8, or three marks. And 5/8 is 1/2 plus 1/8, or five marks. Just measure them out and recount the marks to be sure you've got it right.

Metal rulers and yardsticks are the best made. Wood rulers get nicked as you cut against the edge, and soon you have a ragged edge instead of the straight edge you are trying to draw.

In your measuring set you should have a 12-inch ruler, a yardstick, and a tape measure. Don't rely on a cloth tape measure for accurate measurements— it wrinkles and thus isn't rigid or accurate. Use a laminated plastic tape which can't stretch or wrinkle.

1 inch	=	1/4	or	8/8	or	16/16
3/4 inch	=	3/4	or	6/8	or	12/16
1/2 inch	=	2/4	or	4/8	or	8/16
1/4 inch	=	1/4	or	2/8	or	4/16

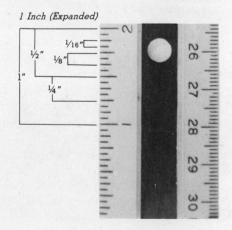

1 Inch (Expanded)

PAPER

An unlimited supply of paper is highly convenient to draw feet, make patterns, and draw sketches. Years ago a friend of ours gave us a box of computer read-out paper, lined on one side and blank on the other. At last we can say something good about the computer. This paper is large (11 by 15 inches), really one long piece with perforations. Ideal for making any size patterns.

Most computer centers have tons of extra paper they throw away and are usually willing to give it to you—free—if you ask. Try to track down a university, a business, or other computer center and get a big boxful.

I don't recommend the use of cardboard for patterns. It is too thick to get a good cutout, too difficult to find, and too much hassle, since you are going to use the pattern only once. Paper bags, of course, work well.

Don't forget to use a pair of old, cheap scissors to cut paper because it dulls good shears.

SANDING AND FINISHING TOOLS

Rougher

Frequently the leather you use is oily or very smooth and will not take or absorb glue easily. To help solve this problem you "rough up" the leather, thus opening the pores and actually getting the fibers "standing up" so that they can provide a better bond with the glue. Ordinary heavy-grit sandpaper does the job quite well. We worked with sandpaper for years without knowing we were missing this

roughing tool. It has little wires shaped so that they rough up or tear the leather and do this preparation job fast. It is handy to have around, but sandpaper works too. Files and other rasping tools are flat, and you need some rounded surface to sand the leather adequately.

Electric Sander

An electrically powered sanding drum is a very, very lovely tool to have to finish your shoes or sandals. You will use it after the shoes are all assembled and quite wearable but still look crude. In assembling everything you join two or more layers of leather and soling together to get the final bottom. No matter how carefully you cut out each individual piece, the edge will always look ragged and rough and uneven. A sanding wheel smooths the edges so that all the pieces look like one even sole, a single unit. Then it can be dyed and the edges polished—burnished—to a high gloss. Suddenly your shoes don't look homemade, but handmade.

You can, of course, sand the edges by hand. Use a wood rasp, made by Surefoam, some sandpaper, and plenty of time. The edge will eventually look fairly decent. It does take time and muscle and doesn't do as well as something electric.

If you aren't willing to invest in a power sander immediately, take the shoes to your neighborhood repair shop and for a fairly minimal fee they will do the sanding for you. The repair shop has an enormous machine, a finisher, with several sanding wheels, burnishing wheels, and vacuum attachments that can turn a botched mess into a thing of beauty. It is, however, fairly easy to make an adequate at-home equivalent.

rougher

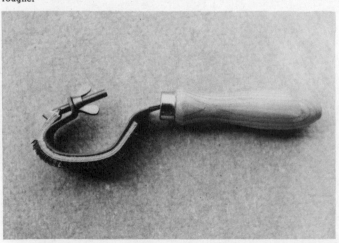

electric sander

If you have an electric drill at home, this can be transformed into a sander. For a few dollars, you can buy a sanding drum attachment. This is sold with several grades of sandpaper shaped in small belts that slip over the drum. The drill motor is a small motor and isn't made to be used for extended periods or under heavy pressure. If you don't already own one, or if you plan to make a lot of shoes or sandals, there is a second alternative that is infinitely superior.

My home "finisher" uses an old ½-horsepower washing machine motor. Considering the number of discarded washing machines around, it shouldn't be much of a problem to find a used motor at a garage sale or junk shop. These motors have a shaft projecting from them that is ideal for our needs. To this shaft attach a work arbor (a connector with threads so that you can then screw on the sanding drum). Just use the standard sanding drum sold. Because soles have curves at the heel, toe, and instep, you do need a drum arrangement rather than a flat surface for sanding. The motor will have to be bolted to a table or a piece of wood that can be clamped to a table, and you may have to buy or build a motor stand. Keep in mind that the drum has to hang over the edge of a table so you can work using the undersection of the drum.

All these parts, including a new motor if you feel wealthy, are sold at Sears or Wards or other catalog stores.

One other important thing: this is filthy, messy work. Sanding reduces the rubber or leather sole to a fine powder which doesn't fall neatly to the ground. It goes everywhere—over your face, your clothes, and most of the room. I have a guard over my drum which keeps a lot of this hideous dust out of the face. I also wear smocks and sometimes goggles and a respirator when I'm doing a lot of work. The dust sprays mainly in front of the wheel and up, so try to set up in a well-lighted corner of the garage or outside on a balcony— never inside if you value your home or cleaning time.

DECORATING TOOLS

Tooling and stamping leather is terribly popular these days, with dozens of shaped stamps available to embellish the leather and decorate it. I never use these stamps. First, they don't work on soft leather. Second, and more important, I put them in the same classification as coloring books, feeling they inhibit your creativity and artistic development. What kind of learning can you possibly experience by pound-

ing a group of predetermined, overused designs into leather? So much of working with leather is work. It must be done in a certain way if the finished product is going to turn out to be well crafted. The decoration part is the art part of arts and crafts and the part in which you can express yourself.

Acrylic paints work very well on sheepskin. Beads brighten up any moccasin and can be used on shoes, boot tops, and so on. Once you've done the hard part, have fun.

Use an ordinary child's woodburning set to design and decorate your shoes before, during, or after assembly. It makes a beautiful, soft line on the leather, is easy and cheap, and doesn't require any elaborate wetting of the leather before it can be used.

If you are not an artist, don't let that dissuade you, here is where you can start to become one. Just start with simple designs, symbols, flowers, or lines in a very simple pattern. When you finish, it will be your effort, your design and accomplishment and not a combination of this stamp and that stamp. After you've burned, fill in areas with colored dyes. Dyes tend to bleed, and the burned line stops and holds the dye where you want it. Using the wood burner is a wonderful way to personalize an item with someone's name. Everyone responds to his own name, and putting it on the item makes it truly the custom gift or purchase that it is. In the beginning shop days when I had plenty of time and few orders, everything that went out of the shop had "Especially Crafted for———" burned on the lining of the shoe or moccasin or the topsole of the sandal. People love it.

HELPFUL TOOLS

Hammers

For general beginning work in shoemaking any old hammer will do. All you are going to use it for is bamming down soles and rivets. The perfect hammer for all-round use is a steel-headed ball-peen hammer, a metalworker's tool. For someone who isn't all muscle, this is well balanced and you can get whatever strength you have fully behind it. I feel more comfortable using it without the claws of a finish hammer looming up in my face. The "ball" end of it is useful for hitting leather you don't want to mark and essential if you are going to set Sam Browne buttons on sandals. Even the handle is useful: you can jam it around the toes of shoes to stretch them out. Leather stores are big on leather mallets. I never use mine.

For nailing, you'll need a tack hammer. An ordinary hardware store tack hammer—$1.95 or so. A tack hammer doesn't have to be heavy to drive in little sandal nails, just balanced. In selecting yours try out every one at the store to see which feels most comfortable. Don't make the beginner's mistake of holding the hammer near the head. Train yourself to hold it at the end of the handle and thus let it deliver all the power it has.

In passing I must mention the French hammer. It looks so professional and crafty, and all the catalogs say it is a must for the shoemaker. Far from it —it is all but useless. The head is angled in such a way that in striking a surface your hand hits the table before the head. You have to use it on the edge of a table. It was designed for shoe repair one hundred years ago and just isn't of value today.

Pliers

DIAGONAL SIDE CUTTERS OR PLIERS. These are very useful in removing rivets and nails. They can cut through the metal of the rivet by prying between the two layers of leather. Pry from the wrong side of the leather so you don't mar the surface.

CHANNEL-LOCK PLIERS. A very useful at-home tool sold at hardware stores. The difference between these and ordinary pliers is that you can vary the size of the opening with channel-lock pliers and lock it into that desired size. Extremely useful in opening stuck glue cans, twisting off the tops of dye bottles, removing old soling on a resole job, and a million other daily tasks.

Anvil

The type of anvil I recommend is merely a piece of scrap steel from a junkyard. You will not need one unless you nail sandals or shoes together. The nails must hit a hard piece of steel to clinch. We have an anvil that is welded to a steel stand and base so that we can sit in front of it and nail, but that isn't necessary. Traditional anvils come in weights from 3 pounds up to 100 pounds, but even the little 3-pounders are hard to find.

Traditional shoemaker's anvils are called lasting jacks and look like a steel foot upside down. I rarely, if ever, use mine because I do not work from the underside of the shoe as shoemakers did in the past. If you plan to do a lot of nailing, try to find a flat piece of steel. Otherwise you can set rivets and do heavy hammering against a solid concrete floor.

HARDWARE

Tacks (Shoemaking Nails)

The points of shoemaking nails differ from ordinary nails. While an ordinary nail merely comes to a

pliers

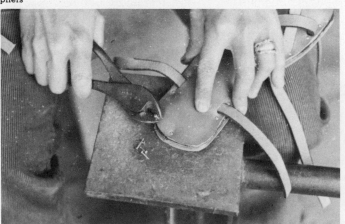

anvil

point, a shoemaker's nail or *clinching* nail has a pinlike point on one side of it, making a curve. This is designed so that the nail will penetrate through all layers of leather and soling, strike the anvil—or something hard—and curl in the direction of the curve. When the pinlike point curls, it will curl back into or *clinch* the leather. Shoemaking nails also have tiny notches in the shank, and the combination of the grip these give and the clinching makes it very, very difficult to remove the nail once it is properly embedded. As you walk on the nail and wear through the metal and leather, the nail continues to be forced into the clinch until you have worn it down to the end of the curve. By that time it is generally time for a resole.

Nails are sold in lengths that vary by ⅛ inch and are referred to in eighths, such as ⅜, ½, ⅝. The length of the nail is critical if the sole is to wear properly. Ideally it should be just a hair longer than the thickness of the portion you are nailing so the point can penetrate and clinch. If the nail is properly placed you should see a fine indentation like a pinprick in the sole bottom. If the nail is too long, too much of the curve will be exposed and the nail will wear out much faster.

Nails are sold in both brass and iron. The brass are better, but hard to find. They are more finely machined, the point is sharper, and they don't rust the way iron nails do.

Nails are sold by the pound and come flat-headed or round-headed. The round-headed are easier to remove. If you are making a shoe or sandal with a midsole of latigo or something thin, you will have to use the flat-headed, very short iron nails, number one, ¼ inch. They are the shortest made.

NAILING. Nail along the edge of the shoe or sandal about 3/16 inch from the edge. The nail should be placed with the curve pointing to the inside. Thus when it clinches it will clinch inward and not come through the side of the sole.

To set the nails use a small tack hammer. Place the nail in the leather—the point will stick so that you don't have to hold it—then lightly tap it with the hammer to set it. Use a sort of sweeping, curving forward motion with the hammer. Then hammer until you think it is through the sole and properly clinched. Check to make certain.

It's really very simple. Just take some practice hits before you start on the real thing. Sometimes you can hit the nail in the wrong way and it flies across the room. It is a good idea to do your nailing in a spot where it won't get someone's eye while you're working.

Myth holds that the old-time shoemakers kept a bunch of nails in their mouth and spat them out as needed. Let's clear this up: they kept wooden pegs in their mouth. Today's nails would be quite dangerous and painful with their pinlike tips pricking the inner lining of your mouth.

Sam Browne Buttons

These "buttons" are unobtrusive, practical, easy-to-use closures for sandal straps. Our customers consistently select them rather than buckles, which seem cumbersome and annoying in comparison. You slip the leather strap over the button and it's on, pop it off and it's off, but it never slips off by itself. An ideal solution for those of us who won't take time to attach buckles or who don't like their heavy look.

Three problems with Sam Browne buttons: hard to find, no jig is sold to set them (you can make one), and only one of four available designs works acceptably. The important difference is in the design and quality engineering. The good one is manufactured by North & Judd and is solid brass, not nickel-plated or nickel. Of the four designs, the shoulder of the North & Judd model is the biggest, the shank is the longest, while the button part is the smallest and the washer that comes with it is made to fit it. The big shoulder is necessary to rest easily on the jig, the long shank to be able to use heavy latigo without skiving and weakening the leather, and small buttons so it won't dig into your foot.

To make the jig, drill a hole in a small metal block (preferable) or a hard piece of hardwood, about ¼ inch in diameter and ½ inch long. The button or head will go into this hole, the shoulder will rest on the edge, and it will thus provide a firm, solid working surface for the hammering.

To set the button, punch a hole the size of the shank in the leather strap about ½ inch from the end of the strap. Put the button face down in the jig, then put the shank through the hole in the leather, then the washer over the leather and shank. Now take the ball end of a ball-peen hammer and strike all around the edges of the tip of the projecting shank until it flattens out and mushrooms over the sides of the washer. The metal is now permanently over the washer and will not come off. A button cannot be reused or reset; it is a one-shot deal. Hit hard and make your anvil sing.

setting Sam Browne buttons

If the resultant mushroomed area is rough, run it over the sanding drum to smooth the metal.

Use your slot punch to make a slot in the leather about ½ inch long. Place it on your sandal on the strap coming out of hole 1.

Although these buttons are more expensive than buckles, the one size fits any strap and you don't have to carry a wide assortment of buckles.

Buckles

Sandal buckles are square or oval with a bar going through the center and a prong attached to the bar. They come in various sizes from ½ inch up (unfortunately none is ⅜ inch). Solid brass is best.

To attach one, simply punch a slot about 1½ inches from the end of the strap coming out of hole 1 on the sandal design. Thread the leather under the back of the buckle, up and over the bar, putting the prong through the slot, and back under the leather so that you have created a loop around the bar, but under the buckle. Make the loop tight, punch holes through both layers of leather about ½

inch back from the end of the bar, and rivet the two layers together. Simple.

Rivets

Rivets are used to join two or more pieces of leather together to attach buckles on narrow straps, or to add decorative tabs and such on shoes. They are a quick and easy method of attachment particularly suited to heavier leather that is too stiff and oily to sew.

The rivet is in two metal pieces—a male and a female—and is hammered together to become permanently joined as a single unit, with the leather between. The medium length, number 2204, is usable for almost any need.

Double-headed rivets look the same on both sides and are best. There is no right or wrong, inside or outside, piece. We use a brass-plated brand that has little indentations to enable you to snap them together temporarily while you take the time to pick up your hammer. A desirable feature.

To use rivets, simply punch two holes—making sure they line up—in the two pieces of leather, put the male piece through the holes, the female piece over it, and snap together. Then put the rivet on the anvil, or some hard surface, and give it several hard whacks with the hammer until the rivet is flattened and the sound of hammering is a dull thud.

Rivets are cheap and easy to use, but any place that you can rivet you can always sew with your stitcher.

Eyelets

Eyelets are a sometimes useful but not essential piece of hardware. They do add reinforcement to the lace hole on shoes and moccasins so the leather cannot stretch, and they give the item a nice little decorative touch.

Setting them requires a special device. Mine looks like a punch, and when squeezed it forces the edge of the eyelet, on the inside of the lace hole, to curl and bend around the leather. All you do is put it in the hole and squeeze. Easy and fun.

After you have your materials and tools together you are ready to begin making shoes or sandals or moccasins. All three begin with a drawing and involve measuring and looking at the feet. The drawing will be utilized in a different way for each type of footwear, but the way you draw the feet is the same. Your shoemaking will properly begin with yourself. You naturally want a pair or several pairs, and you will be the best judge of how well you can follow the directions and make the shoes fit. It will not be long until your family and friends start requesting shoes from you, offering to pay, and you will be discovering the hundreds of varied shoe and foot problems people can have—no, you are not alone—and you will start finding out that there is a lot more to shoes and shoemaking than you had imagined.

Fitting the foot is not as easy as fitting other parts of the body—which isn't easy either. Feet vary widely in shapes, they are incredibly curvaceous, and we depend on them to move us around for an average of seventy years. Shoes are not particularly compatible with feet. In societies that do not wear shoes, foot problems are rare. In our society anyone over age forty can usually contribute something to an aching-foot discussion; so remember that you are making an item that can do serious damage to the person unless it is properly fitted and designed for him.

By way of explaining some of the problems you will be asked to solve, let's look at a few of the customers (family and friends, yourself) you will encounter over the years.

A carpenter will complain that all ready-made boots wear out in two months no matter what he buys. A 200-pound teacher stands on his feet all day, his legs ache, his back hurts, and he needs something special. A woman eighty years old stays healthy by walking a mile a day and she can't get any walking shoes to fit the feet she admittedly distorted by wearing pointed-toe heels in the fifties. A teenager with size 14 feet is off to college and wants one good pair to last him all year. A man with very bony, narrow feet can't find anything that doesn't rub his heel and hurt. A divorcee is changing her life style and moving to Colorado and wants something warm. An eighteen-year-old girl has had polio and always has to buy two pairs of shoes to get a fit. A pregnant housewife says her feet are too wide and her instep too high and she can't get anything comfortable. A young back-to-the-lander apologizes for going barefoot as a teenager and having ugly, wide feet with narrow heels.

All of these people present different, interesting challenges to you. Your shoe customers won't be sedentary TV watchers or cocktail lounge habitués; they will be active workers and doers who need good healthful shoes. They've tried other commercial shoes and are here to see you. Although none of them customarily pays $30 or $50 for shoes, they've made up their minds that it will be well worth it to get the right thing. But what is the right thing?

Since you are using the actual foot to construct the shoe, the right thing will happen almost automatically. The shoe will be wide and long enough for the foot and have plenty of toe room so that the toes can easily flex and bend. Beyond that your only problems will come in selecting the proper soling to suit the individual's body weight and purpose of the shoe and the proper leather or combination of leathers that will give the support the wearer requires, or doesn't require. By support I do not mean arch supports or stiff cardboard fillers that make the shoe unbendable. Far from that, the shoe must be flexible, particularly at the ball of the foot, so that the foot can move and bend as it was designed to do. Foot doctors say we do not need and probably should not have heels of any height on our shoes. They throw the spine out of line, off balance, and can cause back and leg pain. Try to steer your customers away from the heels. Wedges are a better solution if they insist on some elevation, because wedges provide continuous support under the arch area rather than an abrupt rise at the heel.

The overweight teacher, for instance, would be helped by heelless shoes. Overweight people have additional problems because their feet are carrying more poundage than the bones, muscles, and ligaments are structured to carry. The average 150-pound person will put more than 132 tons of weight on his feet in one mile of walking. The feet are designed for this, but overweight puts strain on them and they should have a sole to cushion the impact and leather sturdy enough to resist enormous pressure and strain and keep the foot in place in the shoe.

Normal people and feet do not require arch supports. They help support weak arch muscles, but their presence discourages strengthening of those muscles, and thus eventually the natural muscles atrophy and become dependent on the artificial support. You shouldn't put an arch support in unless the person requests it and is willing to pay just a bit extra to show he is serious. The padding in all your footwear will cushion the bottom of the foot and mold the arch so that no spot receives more strain than another. Usually this padding is more than sufficient for the average person.

Your shoes will almost automatically be durable and will last longer than ready-made shoes and will be made to be repaired easily when they need it. You will use all leather, good leather, for all the uppers and liners and inner linings and reinforcement pieces you put on. Nothing will be of stiff cheap cardboard or canvas or plastic. You will use nylon thread so it cannot rot or rip or tear at the seams or rub or cause corns.

When people say they want a comfortable and durable shoe, it is up to you to interpret what that means to them. The comfort and how the shoes will last is in large measure determined by the structure of a person's foot.

The carpenter, for example, probably has stocky, muscular feet. These are the feet I think of as bulls. They are big, even for the size of the person; they are thick, heavy, tough, solid. Their owners may be quiet, sensitive people, but they walk heavily, they march and tromp and barrel and wear shoes out in two or three months. When these people say they need a durable shoe, nothing is too heavy for them. The toughest soling and leather you have available will be broken in by them easily in days. If they want a work boot, they need two layers of 4- or 6-ounce leather, reinforced with a heavy 24-iron sole. People who have these feet want a heavy fixed-strap sandal design, to hold the foot and withstand the enormous force of pressure they exert. Physically their feet can easily withstand the tight, heavy strapping, but these are the very feet that should not have an arch-strap design, because they will rip the nails out in days (see chapter on sandals). A heavy ⅝-inch continuous strap will not succumb to their overwhelming abuse.

On the other end of the spectrum is the man with bony, narrow feet. When he says comfortable he means he wants a shoe that is loose, will not rub anywhere at any time in any place. These are the tender feet, the thin-skinned highly sensitive individuals who must have something soft above all else. The feet look delicate, bony, generally pasty, because they are always protected. These people don't march around barefoot on gravelly beaches —their feet are too tender, without fat to protect them. These people complain a lot; they are finicky because they have learned that the slightest unevenness in the stitching can cause pain. Thus if they order a heavy-duty work boot you do everything to make a boot that will protect them from weather and injury and hard surfaces, but you try to make the boot light, loose: two layers of leather, one 4-ounce and one of soft deerskin next to the foot, with a sheepskin inner lining. The soling should only be heavy enough to protect them and light enough so that it doesn't give any resistance when the foot is flexed. These people are easy on shoes, walk lightly and softly, and don't need heavy reinforcement. They love soft deerskin and sheepskin and will take care of it. You make them sandals with great reservation, searching for lightweight latigo, soft and stretchy, that will not rub or irritate. These people do not develop calluses which protect the feet; they get blisters. They need a design without a toe strap, so they can wear socks. No soling is too light for them; nothing is too soft or stretchy. They love moccasins.

People with feet that are too wide, or heels too narrow, have feet that are ideal for the custom shoemaker. Many small women have this problem. They will tell you they are hard on shoes, but their real problem is that their wide feet spread the shoe, stretch it beyond its natural limits, and they frequently end up walking on the leather uppers rather than the sole. They are used to all shoes being too tight and hurting or being too long if they go to the next size. When you make the shoe to their foot drawing, their problems will disappear. You don't need to take special precautions for these feet, except to make a shoe that fits well. Your major challenge here is that the feet are small—harder to work on than big size 14 feet—and they curve and change distance and thickness within very short spaces. People with such feet generally walk only on the heel and ball of the feet, the high arch keeping most of the bottom off the ground. Thus the footwear must be designed to stay on. When the heel lifts up to step, two-thirds of the foot actually lifts and can easily walk completely out of the shoe if it is not snug at the heel and tight enough so that it doesn't slop and slap around. The side-opening shoe style is ideal for this foot: it fits well, is snug at the heel and instep, but does not put pressure on the instep. Measurements for moccasins for this foot should be done very carefully and time taken to design a shoe around rises and falls.

All of these foot types and shoe problems are simple. If you feel someone has a problem you are not equipped to handle—fallen arches, for example —suggest he see a foot doctor, who will make devices more complex than you can. Most people know instinctively what they want and what will be comfortable. You must merely listen and offer suggestions. The divorcee going to Colorado first needs a pair of your sheepskin moccasins. She'll love them. The gal who had polio simply needs two shoes, each one with its own pattern. In making them for her, don't try to do a favor by attempting to even the two up so they are closer to the same size. The difference in size will not be obvious if each shoe fits its foot well, but it will be very obvious—and the shoes will be uncomfortable—if you try to distort the reality: that the two feet are not alike. What you can try to do is draw the toe shapes so that at a quick glance they look the same.

The eighty-year-old woman is no problem. In molding the shoes you will stretch the leather over her hideously deformed toes that overlap each other and provide the freedom and space they need for comfortable walking. The shoes will probably not be "pretty" because they will bulge up in strange places. They should be pretty to her because at long last they will fit. If she tries to have you make them just a bit narrower or a bit more stylish, like commercial shoes, you must refuse. You cannot make something for her that is both stylish and fits correctly. Style should be last on your list, below fit and craftsmanship. If her priorities are in a different order, you are not the person to help her.

DRAWING THE FEET

Since all footwear starts with the foot drawing and the accuracy of your fit depends on this drawing, you should take time to draw the feet carefully and examine them and think about the shoes you are making. People love the personal attention of the individual foot drawing, but they still feel an embarrassed self-consciousness about having a friend or a total stranger crawling around intensely scrutinizing their naked feet. During the drawing their feet are cold and your pen tickles and there is a strong inclination on your part to get it over with so that the embarrassment is not prolonged. Don't rush yourself. Care and thoroughness at this beginning point will save you a tight-chested, sweaty-palm, cigarette-in-each-hand anxiety at the time of delivery when you find out if all of your work and planning has been right.

There are a few do's and don'ts to remember about foot drawing.

Don't draw your own feet if you are making a pair of shoes for yourself. You tend to move your feet to accommodate yourself and you can get a very inaccurate outline of your own foot.

Don't use the same drawing or pattern twice, even for the same person, for the same item. Anything new you begin should start with a fresh frame of mind and a new look. Shoes, sandals, and moccasins, which all start with the same drawing, are made into completely different sole patterns. Thus, if you plan to make someone both shoes and moccasins, draw the foot twice. It takes only seconds.

Don't draw the feet with socks on. You need an accurate drawing of the actual feet without the distortions socks can cause.

Try to draw both feet side by side, so you can compare them later on. Use paper large enough so you can do the drawing side by side.

Always use a ball-point pen to do the drawing. Don't use a felt-tipped pen or a crayon or anything that makes a thick line or is very thick itself. A ball-point pen line adds about $\frac{1}{16}$ inch. A pen line plus half the thickness of the pen shaft is about $\frac{1}{8}$ inch, so your drawing, with the extra $\frac{1}{8}$ inch all around the foot, is actually $\frac{1}{4}$ inch larger and longer than the foot. A felt-tipped pen is even thicker and would create a drawing much larger than the actual foot. Don't use a pencil—you will be marking over and around this drawing to make your sole pattern. Ball-point ink is permanent, and you will be able to erase your pattern marks without erasing the original drawing.

To do the drawing, have the person stand with his full weight distributed evenly on both feet, standing

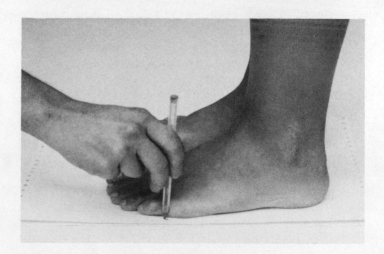

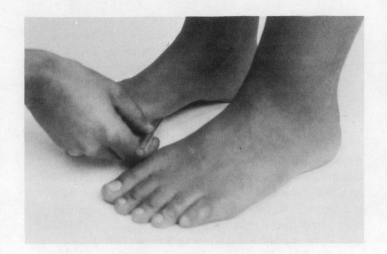

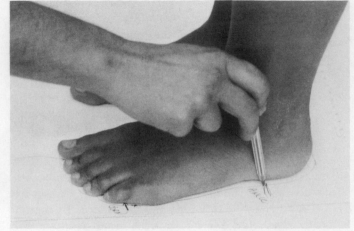

normally. Make sure the person does not move his feet, toes, legs, or knees while you are drawing. People tend to move their toes and squinch them up so that they don't look so large. Make them keep still.

Draw around the outsides of both feet, always keeping your pen perpendicular (straight up and down) to the paper. It can be tricky to get a smooth continuous drawing around the heel. Make as many marks as you must to get the general contours, trying to keep the pen perpendicular. If you must tip the pen in order to avoid the calf, do so. Just be careful that you do not angle the pen so that it draws underneath the heel instead of around it.

When you finish drawing around the feet, draw under them, so you know how high or deep the arch is. Just slide the pen underneath the arch until you touch flesh. The foot has many curves and does not touch the ground where it appears to. Your arch drawing may extend from under the heel to way above the ball of the foot.

Mark where the anklebones are. They are not

opposite each other, and later you might want to know where they are. Keeping your pen perpendicular, make a mark on the paper where the center of each bone is.

Indicate on the drawing any corns or bunions.

One other thing about feet. Many people stand with their weight rolled on the outsides of their feet. Watch for this when you are drawing. If a person isn't standing squarely on his full foot, your sole pattern will come out looking as if the feet are hooked. Very few people actually have such a hook. Don't make up a shoe with this hook in it. It will not fit.

MEASURING

Use a tape measure and measure the height of the toes. This will be useful in making the moccasin pattern.

Using a tape measure, measure all the way around the ball of the foot at the widest point. This measurement is used in creating the shoe upper

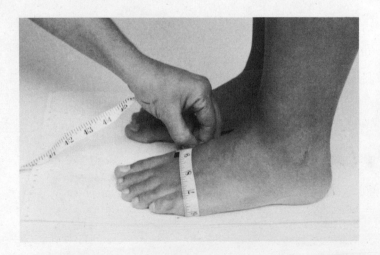

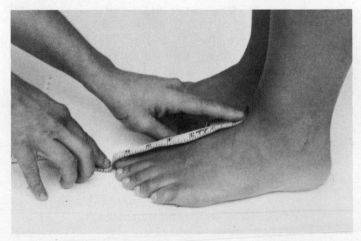

pattern. It is very important in children's footwear, since the size of their feet is always deceptive, particularly when you are looking at the flat drawing.

Finally, measure the length of the foot from the instep where it meets the leg to the end of the longest toes. Have the person lift his foot and write all your measurements within the outline of the foot drawing. You will soon be cutting away all of the outside paper, and if these measurements are written there they'll be lost.

LOOKING AT AND COMPARING FOOT DRAWINGS

For any of the footwear you make, these foot drawings will be used to draw a sole pattern, the pattern from which you will make the sole of the shoe or moccasin or sandal. Each kind of footwear differs in the amount of toe room, space for the heel, and so on, and instructions will be given in detail in the chapter covering each kind of shoe. However, you should approach the sole pattern and the way you look at the foot drawing in the same way.

The foot drawing won't look like much: a curvy outline of a foot with five lumps where the toes are, lines indicating the arch area and the ankles, and two bumps showing the balls of the feet. It isn't much, but it's all you will need to make your shoes. If it is correct, it will look slightly bigger than the actual foot because of the pen line. This is taken into account when we make the sole pattern.

Only by working with several feet will you begin to understand how different they really can be. To appreciate the difference between feet, find two or three people with feet supposedly the same size as your own—7½ or whatever. Draw their feet, compare the drawings, and see how much variation there is despite the fact that a shoe salesman will claim they are the same. Your challenge when you make shoes will be to follow the basic shape of this foot outline and take into account individual peculiarities to develop a nice shape for the shoe, one that flatters the foot but fits it.

The foot is divided into four basic areas: the toes, the ball, the arch-instep, and the heel. A charting of this division is included (see page 32) to help train your eye to see on flat paper what is so obvious on the three-dimensional foot.

TOE AREA. Shaping the toe area will present the most difficulty for you in your pattern work. Several examples of toes, the regular and irregular shapes, and how I have dealt with them are included throughout the moccasin and shoe chapters to help

you. Frequently, if you follow the exact shape of the toes, you will end up with ridiculous-looking shoes. The important thing to remember is that the toes should not be restricted.

BALL AREA. The ball area is the widest point on the foot. If the shoe is not wide enough here it will be painful. The ball receives so much use—and abuse—that the shoe must fit exactly at this point and not be too tight.

Between the ball of the foot and the toes above it there will appear to be an indentation where the foot curves in from the toe and out again to the ball. At no time should you ever follow this indentation in creating your pattern. First, of course, it would make an absurd-looking shoe sole. More important, the foot does move within the shoe and if the sole were indented there, the foot would be walking on leather at times rather than soling.

ARCH-INSTEP AREA. Most of it is hollow space. A shoe or moccasin will fit better if you design the sole pattern so that the leather hugs the side of the arch as much as possible and follows the arch's natural contours. On the outside of the foot this area is mostly flesh and fat, little bone. Therefore, in creating the sole patterns you may take great liberties with the lines of your foot drawing and ignore the many lumps and bumps that appear on this side. Most patterns can be drawn with a straight line going from the heel to the ball of the little toe.

HEEL AREA. Heels are very fleshy and malleable. Most are not nicely rounded, but in working with and making shoes it is a good idea to round and shape the heel so that it appears round.

Comparing the Two Feet

Before you turn to one of the specific chapters on moccasins, shoes, or sandals, you should measure and compare the two feet you are working with. With a ruler, measure them to see how long they are from toe to heel and how wide they are at the ball. Expect most people's feet to differ slightly. If there is much more than ¼-inch difference between them, you should make two separate patterns. If you are not sure, draw two sole patterns, one for each foot, cut them out, and compare them. See if there is a noticeable variation between the two. After you have compared the two outlines, select the better drawing and use that foot for the remainder of the pattern work. It is impossible to tell you which one is going to be better. Use the one that most closely

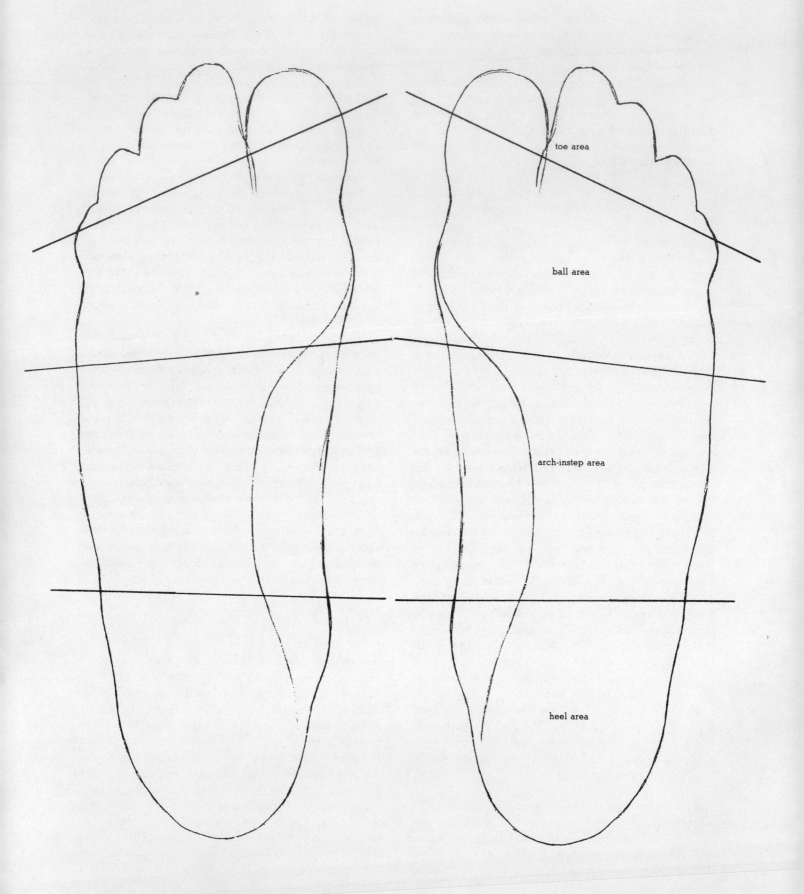

toe area

ball area

arch-instep area

heel area

resembles the foot and gives you the best idea of its actual shape. If you decide to use both patterns, lay one over the other and shape the toes so they are the same.

Generally, you'll make just one pattern, flipping it over for the opposite foot. It is much easier, less confusing, and the left and right will look like a pair. As a matter of course, I usually draw the right foot because if a person is right-handed it is generally the larger, more developed foot.

Once you have compared the feet and selected the one you will use in your patternwork, you are ready to begin whatever you've chosen to make.

CHILDREN'S FEET

In many ways our shoe manufacturers have unwittingly devised for us instruments of torture no less destructive or sadistic than the Chinese custom of binding women's feet to keep them small. These torture instruments are particularly terrible for children: their fat, malleable, and jellylike feet have mistakenly been shoved into rigid little boxes that allegedly give them the support they lack. These so-called support shoes merely tend to prevent the child from using his feet and from developing the very muscles, ligaments, and tendons that will give him the lifelong natural support he needs to go without artificial assistance. According to foot specialists, most children need only protective footwear: loose socks, very flexible shoes or moccasins, and absolutely no support anywhere. Bare feet are best. Most children, toddlers, need socks or shoes only when they need mittens.

Children instinctively do not like you to fuss around their feet and most will give you a lot of resistance when you try to draw them. This is particularly true with preschoolers, for whom moccasins are just about the only footwear they need or that you can make for them. Be sure to draw as accurately as their wiggling will allow. You are dealing with small proportions, which are much more difficult to work with. Your pen and the line will add much more width, proportionately, to the size of their little foot than to an adult's. Your pen will have added ¼ inch, and for a child that is immense in proportion to his foot. All the growing room he will need.

Be sure to measure the height of the toes, around the ball, top of instep to toes, and at the heel, the Achilles tendon (where the bend behind the heel is). You'll not be able to use any standard measurements on any of the footwear, so you must know what the foot dimensions are for that child, at that moment, and plan to make whatever they are now, not a month from now.

When a child is under five his foot is much fatter than it appears on the drawing. As his feet grow, they seem to lengthen without proportional change in thickness around the ball. Thus a ten-year-old may appear to have a foot the same length as his mother's, but it hasn't developed the bulk of the adult foot; it is not carrying the same weight as the mother's. Your problem will be to keep from coming up with a shoe too small for the toddler and too large for the preteen. Do measure, so you will be accurate. After the child is twelve or so, his foot is nearly the same as an adult's and can be treated as an adult foot, but be sure you don't make anything that will restrict its freedom of movement or harm the growth during these final years of development.

Moccasins

A moccasin is a shoe that has one continuous piece of leather underneath the foot and is joined or gathered on the top of the foot: the gathered-toe design. Don't hold on to the idea that a moccasin is only a soft baggy thing that breaks down at the heel and is useful as around-the-house footwear on your day off. It can be anything you want it to be. You are designing for your needs, your life style, and your feet, and an enormous selection of materials is available to you.

The moccasin design in the following pages is based on one that an American Indian woman got from her mother, who got it from her mother, and so on back through the generations. There is only one basic design for moccasins in this book, the gathered-toe design, which was originally developed by the mountain Indian tribes and had a flap that could be turned up as the wearer walked through the dense underbrush. This basic design has evolved today into an enormously diversified category of footwear. You can see it in such commercial shoes as the traditional penny loafer or in the popular boating shoes. Anything can be made from it, from a slip-on soleless slipper to a double-layered, reinforced, double-soled hiking boot.

While there are many interesting, original Indian designs for moccasins, they all have one thing in common: it is extremely difficult to achieve a good reliable fit consistently, if at all, with them. The best-looking moccasins or shoes are worthless if they do not fit. I believe it is best to learn to make —and then modify—one style that will consistently fit very, very well. It is a challenge just to get that consistent fit with one design. The thing that makes it the challenge is that you must create a paper pattern which will result in a moccasin that wraps around and covers the foot exactly, without the benefit of the real foot over which to stretch the leather (as you can with a shoe) or tighten the straps (as you can with a sandal). You must precalculate exactly every rise and fall in the foot before you begin the construction. So if you are a purist and had hoped to find within these pages all the authentic original Indian styles, you might be disappointed. If you want to learn to master one design and endless variations of that design, this moccasin section is what you seek.

For your first moccasin don't start with anything complex. Start with a basic: one layer of leather and a thin rubber or thin leather sole. Be sure to use some sort of soling, or the moccasin will wear out too rapidly. First complete the pattern and make up the moccasin to the point where you are ready to attach the laces. Then you can think about adding a small top or cutting it down or adding decoration pieces or beads. You will be more informed at that point and will understand how all the pieces fit together, and will understand the changes you can make.

A moccasin certainly requires more time and leather and more meticulous attention to detail— particularly in the beginning when you are doing the patternwork—than a shoe or sandal. The more of them you make, the more interesting the patternwork will become for you. Eventually it is the truly fun, exciting, and challenging part of the work, although at this point in your career it may seem to you to be boring or perhaps a greater challenge than you are prepared to undertake. You want to get on with the fun part of it, and sitting around a table drawing lines and thinking in terms of an eighth of an inch doesn't strike you as the crafty experience you had in mind. Nevertheless, the patternwork must be done before you can do the craftwork. This isn't a kit.

Please don't make the mistake of dashing off the pattern. Some of the students wouldn't pay much attention to the instructions. They whipped out something quickly, seemingly without thinking about or caring or understanding what they were doing. Even though the craftwork sometimes turned out to be flawless—say, the lacing on the toe was beautiful—it made absolutely no difference: their pattern had been imperfectly designed, so the moccasins turned out to fit imperfectly. Such students were terribly disappointed and tended to dismiss the entire craft on the basis of their one faulty attempt, whereas the problem was that they had not taken the time to construct the pattern carefully.

Over the years we have developed some standard measurements for basic patternwork on adult moccasins. These measurements work very well for most feet and most moccasin styles. Their beauty is that they will enable you to create your initial pattern easily and without any hassle. Once you understand the function of the pattern pieces—there are three—and their place in the whole moccasin, you will be able to design future patterns easily for anyone, for any purpose, and using any combination of materials.

Your goal in designing a pattern is to have your end product look and fit exactly as you envisioned it in the beginning without having to make any modifications during the construction. Many people never need or want to make any changes at any point. They are completely delighted with everything about their moccasins and consider them to be the most comfortable things they have ever had on their feet.

But anything standard has its drawbacks. So if you are a perfectionist or have very small or very large feet, basing the pattern on the measurements of the foot rather than the standard measurements will be far more practical and satisfying in the end. But don't disregard the basic measurements I will be presenting. They have worked for years, and any drastic departure from them should be taken with care and consideration. Remember, a foot is not very big. A fourth of an inch represents almost a full size difference. Hence, if you make the foot pattern a fourth of an inch longer, you are expanding the moccasin almost a full size.

Definitions of perfect fit vary considerably. What is perfect for one person might be hopelessly sloppy for another. Some like a moccasin to fit so loosely that they virtually walk out of it on every other step, while others like a fit so tight that the moccasin looks like a vise squeezing the circulation out of the foot. These individual likes and dislikes are the challenges you will meet in creating for yourself or for others. It has taken years to figure out

these measurements and the solutions to the vagaries of fit. So let's get on with them, and later get into the ifs and thens.

PATTERNMAKING

There will be three pieces to your final basic pattern: the sole pattern (A), the bottom pattern (one piece made up of B, C, D, and E), and the tongue pattern (F). See below for how these pattern pieces will be joined together to create the completed moccasin. Part A, the sole, covers and attaches to the middle of the bottom pattern. Part B on the bottom pattern will curve up and over your toes and will be sewn to the tongue piece, part F. The two C parts will become the sides of the moccasin. The two D parts will be sewn together, making a center seam at the heel of the moccasin. Part E is a tab that covers the seam and adds protection and reinforcement to the heel.

All these parts may seem confusing to you. Study the pictures until you feel you have the relationships in mind. You should say "eureka" fairly rapidly. It's very simple once you get it.

The Sole Pattern

The sole pattern will be used, by itself, for the sole of the moccasin, the padding, and the inner lining (which covers the padding and goes next to your foot).

The sole pattern is also the basis for the other two pieces, the bottom and the tongue, and must be accurate. If it is inaccurate, they will be too. So take the time and care necessary to get it right.

The sole pattern is created by penciling a line around the foot drawing (see pages 29–30). Get the

Parts of a Moccasin

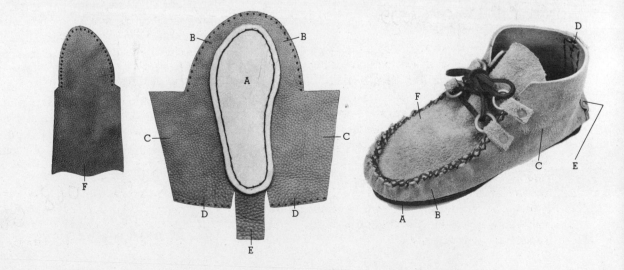

A = sole pattern

B, C, D, E = bottom pattern

B = toe

C = sides

D = back

E = tab

F = tongue pattern

drawing, sit at a table, and have handy a ruler, a pencil, and some large pieces of paper.

Your goal is to make the sole pattern the general shape of the wearer's foot. Few feet are so conveniently shaped that they assume the look of a conventional sole when you make a pattern. Here is an outline of a foot that is just such a shoemaker's delight. Your challenge in creating the sole pattern will be to follow the basic shape and work around individual peculiarities to develop a nice shape, one that is curved and rounded, has no angles, and has generally pleasant, flowing lines.

Because I cannot see the foot you are working with, I can only give you general guidelines for each area of the foot. Read the following hints, analyze the examples, and go to it. You can play with the drawing, subtracting $1/16$ inch here, softening a sharp curve there, and so on.

TOE AREA. This toe area is the trickiest to shape. Several examples are given here to help you. The basic moccasin is very light, it moves and flexes with the foot, and the leather stretches, so it is unnecessary and undesirable to allow more than $1/8$ inch of toe room beyond the longest toe. The smaller toes—the third or fourth—will have a great deal more room than $1/8$ inch, but the longest one must have at least that much.

Four Ways to Shape Sole Pattern Around Toes
(The solid lines are for shoes; the dotted lines are for moccasins.)

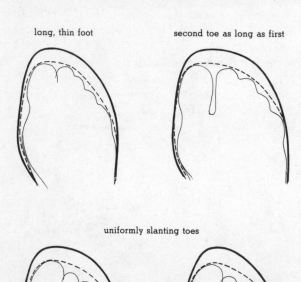

long, thin foot

second toe as long as first

uniformly slanting toes

BALL AREA. Keep to the lines of the foot exactly. No more and no less. Around the outside ball of the foot—behind the little toe—bring the pattern out to the widest point. Don't follow the indentation.

ARCH-INSTEP AREA. Because of the hollow here, the moccasin will tend to bag if you don't make the sole pattern slightly smaller than the drawing. When the moccasin is complete, you will want the leather to cling to the curves of the hollow of your arch.

On the inside of the foot, after following the perimeter of the ball, bring the pattern line inside the foot drawing line at the arch by at least $1/8$ or $1/4$ inch, even if the person who will wear the moccasin is flat-footed. Follow the natural arch line. Start curving back out to the drawing line after you pass the anklebone.

On the outside of the foot around the arch area there may be minor lumps and bumps. Ignore them. They are flesh, very flexible, and your foot does not need to have each one taken into account in order to be comfortable.

HEEL AREA. The heel area should be given some—about $1/8$ inch—extra room all the way around. The heel is fleshy, and you may not need to use that extra $1/8$ inch, but have it anyway. Most heels are not evenly shaped; some come to a point in the back. Reshape the pattern so that the shape is round and pleasant. This will be an asset later on when you are making the moccasin.

When you feel you have made a good pattern, cut it out, making sure to cut smoothly and evenly.

Turn over the completed cutout and look at it from the opposite side. Look at it from a standpoint of shape; look for sharp angles and weird bulges. If you find either, cut off minute pieces until the finished pattern looks like the sole of a shoe. If you have jagged edges in the paper pattern you cut out, these jagged edges will become increasingly more noticeable as you cut from leather.

Finally, the wearer should step on the drawing and see if it fits under the foot without showing paper for more than about $1/8$ inch around the edges. Sometimes, despite all the meticulous measuring and drawing, the foot pattern simply comes out too large. Mark the area where you see too much paper, then very carefully cut away the excess.

The Moccasin Bottom Pattern

ESTABLISHING THE BALL LINE. Using the sole pattern you just made, you will now make the moccasin

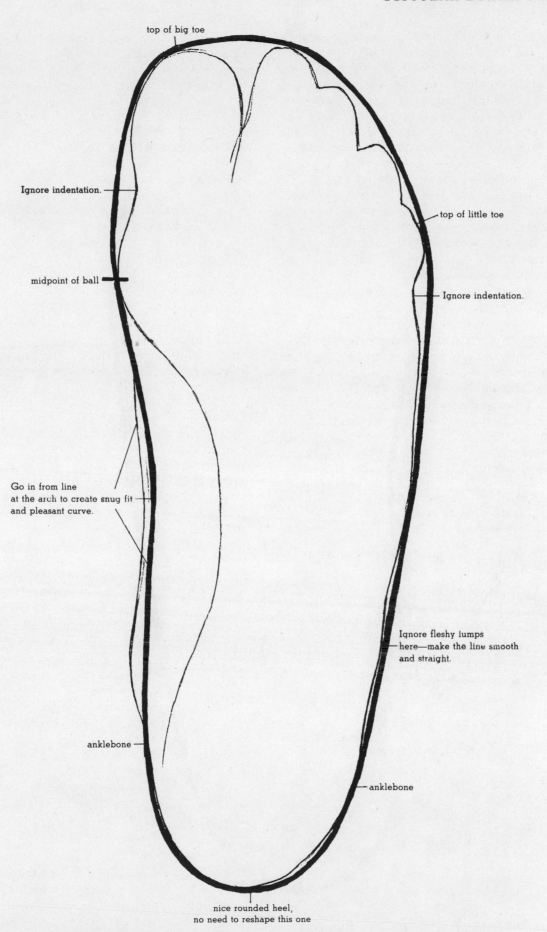

top of big toe

Ignore indentation.

top of little toe

midpoint of ball

Ignore indentation.

Go in from line
at the arch to create snug fit
and pleasant curve.

Ignore fleshy lumps
here—make the line smooth
and straight.

anklebone

anklebone

nice rounded heel,
no need to reshape this one

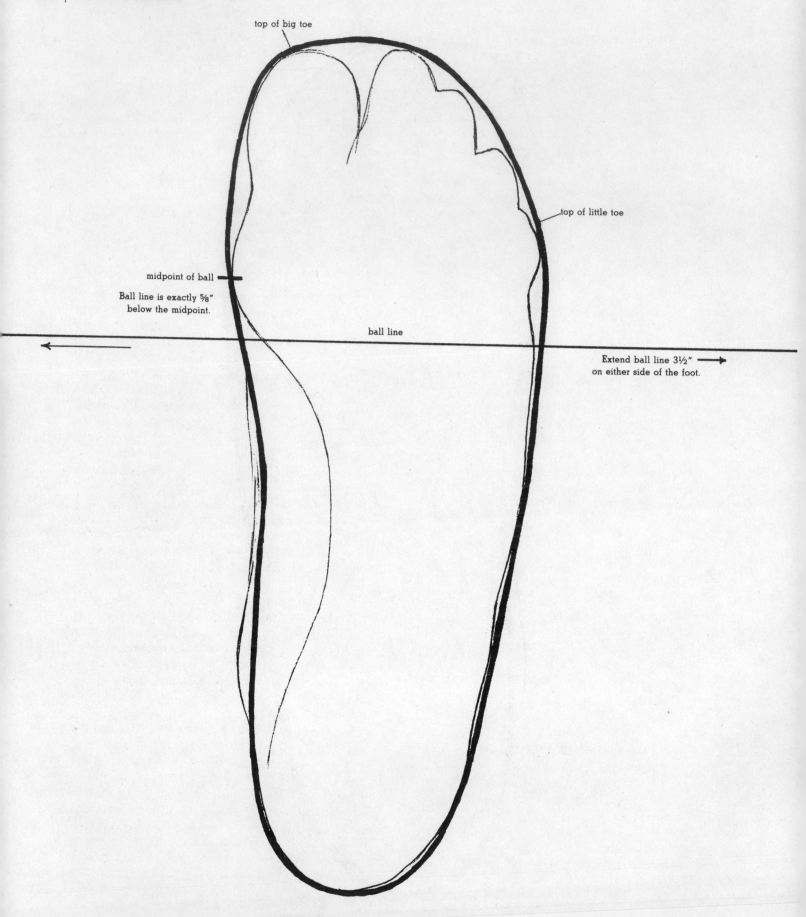

top of big toe

top of little toe

midpoint of ball

Ball line is exactly ⅝"
below the midpoint.

ball line

Extend ball line 3½"
on either side of the foot.

bottom pattern. This pattern, when transferred to leather, will become most of the moccasin. To create the toe (part B) of the moccasin bottom pattern, you must establish the ball line which divides part B from part C.

To begin your pattern and establish the ball line, put the sole pattern on a large piece of paper and trace around it with a ball-point pen. Leave your pattern in place for the moment and look at the ball of the foot: the large lump of flesh and bone right behind the big toe. This is the widest and thickest portion of your foot, and if the shoe is to fit well, it has to be wide enough here. If the moccasin is to stay on your foot, it has to tighten up right behind the ball. It is at this point, right behind the ball, that you establish what I call the ball line. Ahead of the ball line you will allow enough material to cover the thickness of the foot and the toes, and behind the line you will place the material to which the laces that will tie the moccasin on to your foot will be attached.

Try to find the widest, thickest portion of this lump, the ball, and make a small mark there. Now, with your pattern still on the paper, measure down toward the heel from this mark exactly ⅝ inch and make another mark. This lower mark is where your ball line will be drawn across the foot and paper. Using a ruler, draw a line straight across the sole pattern at the mark and extend the line at least 3½ inches beyond the sides of the foot outline. You have now established the ball line. Draw it on the sole pattern too.

TOE AREA.

Marking the toes. While your sole pattern is still on the paper, take a moment to mark the spots on the paper where the top of your big toe is and where the top of the little toe is. This is not an exact spot, just the general location where the toes start to thin out. These marks will be used in helping you create the toe area.

Drawing the toe area. Your goal in creating the toe area (part B) is to reduce the amount of the material above the ball line gradually so that you have the most at the ball and the least around the toes. There must be enough to go over the height of the foot, and, at the ball, to cover the bone on top of the foot. The measurements I have allowed will fit nearly everybody except children, although you may later want to make minor modifications for yourself when the moccasin is well under way.

Along the ball line on either side of the foot, make a mark 1½ inches out from the edge of the

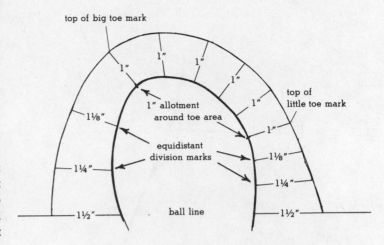

foot. This 1½-inch measurement is correct for almost all people. Now we are gradually going to reduce the amount of leather from this point where the foot is thickest to the toe area where the foot is thinnest. Between the mark you made indicating the top of the big toe and the ball line make two equidistant marks. Do the same on the little-toe side—that is, divide each area into three smaller sections.

Bring the line out to 1¼ inches at the mark nearest the 1½-inch mark at the ball line. The marks nearest the 1½-inch marks should be 1¼ inches away from the foot. The next set of marks should be 1⅛ inches from the foot. The line around the remaining area between the toe marks should be 1 inch from the foot. Now connect all the marks in a smooth and even line. If you have to change the measurements slightly in order to create a smooth line, do so. This might be necessary particularly on the little-toe side, where the distance decreases abruptly and is short.

On the ball line again, mark both sides 2 inches out from your 1½-inch marks and draw the lines out to these marks. The total length of the line on each side of your foot should now be 3½ inches. These extra 2 inches allow enough leather to come up and meet in the middle of the instep. This will probably be cut down at a later date, but you want to allow enough leather so that you can wait and see the moccasin on your foot before deciding what to cut away.

HEEL AREA. Creating the heel of the moccasin bottom pattern (parts D and E) is difficult for some students. Until you have done it, it is somewhat confusing to understand what is being done and why.

I'll try to explain the theory and then get on with the "how-to" part. The moccasin pattern is flat. Your heel and foot are very curvaceous. It presents a

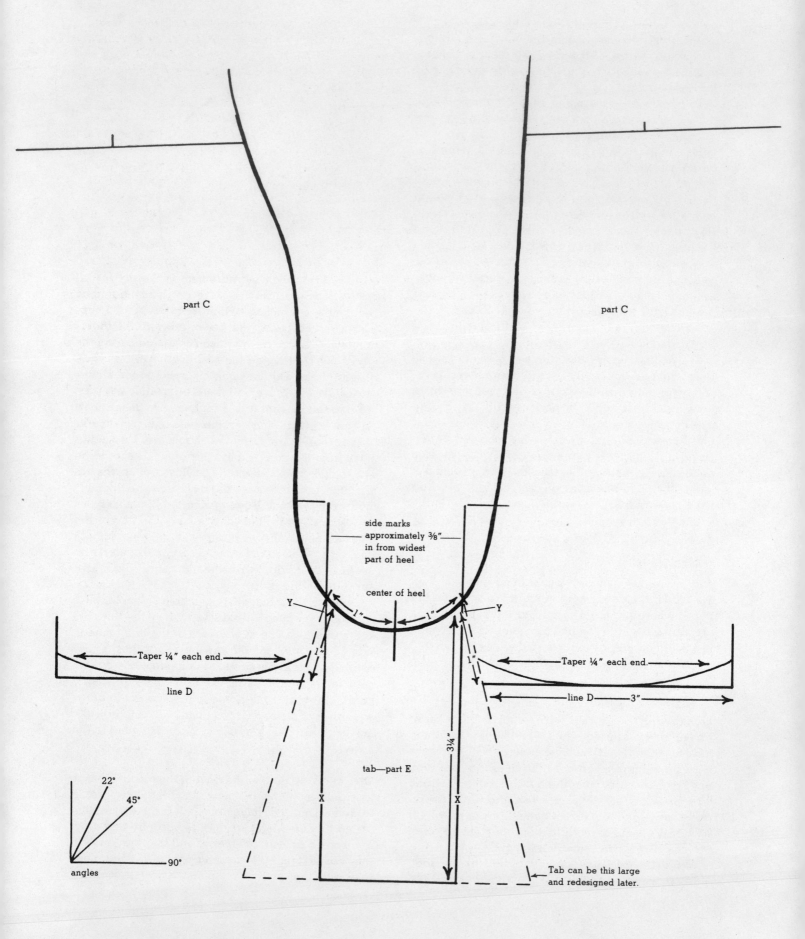

part C

part C

side marks
approximately ⅜"
in from widest
part of heel

center of heel

Y

Y

1"

1"

Taper ¼" each end.

Taper ¼" each end.

line D

line D 3"

1"

1"

3¼"

tab—part E

X

X

22°

45°

90°

angles

Tab can be this large
and redesigned later.

problem to create a heel pattern that will, as much as possible, follow the curve of your heel and not be squared off, as so many moccasins are.

Many moccasins are made so that the leather (and pattern) are split at the center and then sewn up at the back and along the edge near the sole. People walk through the stitching and leather of this seam in no time flat.

You'll use a "tab" (part E) arrangement at the back which covers up the seam at the back, adds needed reinforcement at the heel, and provides waterproofing and dustproofing. Mainly it eliminates that seam at the edge of the sole, where there is a lot of wear.

To provide material for this tab, you have to divide the leather at some point along the curve of your heel, and extend it so that it will meet in the middle of the heel to be sewn together for the back seam.

Make a mark at the center of the heel. If you followed directions on the sole pattern you will have a heel pattern that is round and evenly shaped, with an easily discernible center (see opposite page). Now get a tape measure or a string. Don't use a ruler—it is next to impossible to measure off an inch of curve with a straight line. With the tape on its edge measure 1 inch along the curve of your heel from the center mark on both sides, and make a mark on the foot outline. These are the points at which you will divide the leather. Draw a line 3¼ inches straight back from the heel at both of these points (lines X), then from the points where this line meets the outline of the foot measure a 22-degree angle (angle Y) from the tab lines and draw a 1-inch line on either side. The angle isn't absolutely critical, but it works the best for me.

Now you are practically finished. At the farthest point from the foot along the 1-inch line draw another line 3 inches long going straight out from the sides of the foot (line D). This 3-inch line is the height that most people need for the backs of their moccasins. It is the distance from the floor to a point a bit above the start of the Achilles tendon, the bend at the back of your heel. A commercial moccasin or shoe is less than 3 inches, but these shoes are not heavily reinforced and they need that height in order to stay on and be comfortable. It can always be cut down and modified if you find it is too high, but try this for the first pair.

Connect the 3-inch line at the heel and the 2-inch mark at the ball line to create part C. And the pattern takes shape.

Two more things to do. One: It is necessary to taper the material along line D, your 3-inch line.

Your foot tapers both above and below the tendon (or the tendon sticks out, whichever way you prefer), so the heel of the moccasin should also be tapered. Measure ¼ inch back toward the foot from the 1-inch mark at line X on each side and draw a curve which goes up ¼ inch at both ends of line D and touches line D in the middle.

Two: The tab. The tab can be any shape, just so it is wide enough to cover the stitching up the back. The higher it is, the more reinforcement you will have. The tab actually can be any shape within the angular cut. Students have created very original shapes using parts of this area. You can bring the lines of the tab straight back as in my drawing. However, if you leave the entire area open you can play with the shape later on. To form the tab, connect the two 3¼-inch lines (lines X) you make going straight back from the heel.

That is it for the moccasin bottom part of the pattern. A quick and easy tongue pattern and you'll be ready to start working with the leather. This first pattern you make takes the most time. After you get the hang of it and know what you are going to do, it will only take you about five or ten minutes. So don't give up.

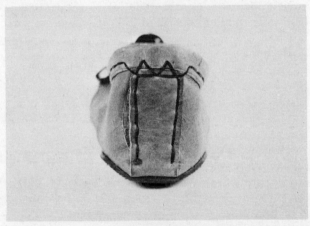

1. Trace around foot pattern from ball line to ball line.

2. Measure in from trace ⅜" all the way around.

3. Connect measuring lines.

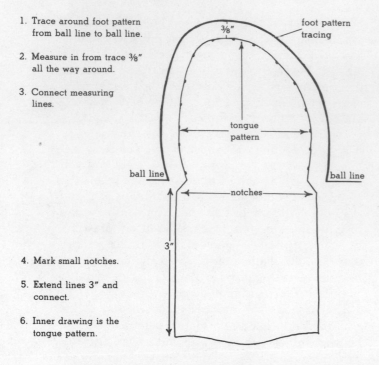

4. Mark small notches.

5. Extend lines 3" and connect.

6. Inner drawing is the tongue pattern.

The Moccasin Tongue Pattern

This is very easy.

Your tongue pattern is actually nothing more than a slightly smaller version of your sole pattern from the ball line up.

Go back to your sole pattern and put it on a fresh piece of paper. Remember when you drew the ball line across the paper with the sole pattern on it? Okay, that ball line should be on the sole pattern. Trace around the pattern from one end of the ball line to the other around the toe. Measure *in* from the tracing ⅜ inch all the way around and connect your measurement marks.

Now you only have to make the "tongue" part of the pattern piece. This section will cover your instep, and most of it will be covered by the sides of the moccasin. It is really only for protection and to cover a bit of the top of your foot.

Lay the tongue pattern over the moccasin bottom pattern and draw little lines down at an angle from the edges of your new, inner line to form sort of notches that match the notches at the ball line of the bottom pattern. Then draw lines straight back toward the heel on both sides about 3 inches long. The purpose of the notches, and thus the additional material, is to fill in whatever small gaps may be in the moccasin at that jointure and prevent small pebbles and dust from entering the shoe. You will probably end up cutting some of this 3 inches down, but at this point you don't have any idea how much you

will want to eliminate and it is so much easier to cut away than to add on.

Cut out all your patterns, making sure you cut carefully and follow the lines. Make especially sure to cut in at the heel, where you made your angle Y.

ASSEMBLING THE MOCCASIN

When your pattern is complete, you are ready to get on with the fun part of the work and start feeling crafty.

Look at your hide and select the appropriate portion of it for your moccasins and the inner linings (see pages 8–9). The grain side is definitely better to have next to your foot; although the suede side appears to be softer and more velvety, it will also rub and irritate your foot and it will be particularly annoying when your foot perspires. Place your patterns on the leather, draw around them with a ballpoint pen, then *flip them over* and draw around them again. Cut them out carefully and smoothly.

The soling and padding should be cut out now as well. You get the maximum out of your soling material if you place your sole pattern on the edge of the sheet of soling, draw around it, then flip the pattern over and place it next to the first outline with the toe of one beside the heel of the other. Don't forget to flip the pattern; there is little you can do with two right feet.

When everything is cut out, dye the edges of the leather if you want to. Do the dying in some part of the house where spillage won't matter. Hold the leather so that the suede side is facing you. In that way any runs will dribble into the suede—usually—and not onto the grain side, where it really can show and ruin the item.

Now is the time to mark your holes in the bottom and tongue.

Marking and Punching Holes
for the Bottom and Tongue

Some time before you sew the moccasins at the toe, holes will have to be punched and marked so that you can sew through them. This can be done at any time prior to the sewing, but it is easiest before you have added the bulk of padding and soling and when the bottom is still flat.

When you see the elaborate procedure for marking the holes, you'll feel I'm too picky and finicky. However, I have good reasons.

To sew up the moccasin toe you must have the same number of holes in the bottom piece as you have in the tongue piece. Without some sort of system, you can become hopelessly lost and confused "just throwing in a bunch of holes." The pieces are not the same size, nor are they the same shape or even symmetrical, so you can't just lay one over the other, or fold one side against the other, or even use a previously made pattern as a guide. All these shortcuts have been tried, and they just don't work. You end up with leather so marked up you have no idea which pen mark means what, or you end up with a bunch of extra holes, or with holes added at odd spots in order to make everything come out even. The holes must match on each piece, and they should be evenly spaced. Please believe me, this system works and saves you hours of frustration.

The more holes you can put in—the closer your stitches are—the more professional looking your moccasins will be. Fewer holes mean a baggier, lumpier look. I finally arrived at 33 being the magic number of holes to use. More could easily be put in the bottom piece, but the tongue piece is only so big and won't take many more.

Plan to use the very smallest hole your revolving punch makes: number 0.

Here's the system—pathetically elementary, but if you don't follow it you'll have problems.

The system is merely a matter of dividing the leather into equal parts five times. Five. Keep track of the number of divisions and you'll always end up with the right number of holes: 33. Count them. The diagrams show much more clearly than I can tell, so follow them.

The only difficulty you'll have is in establishing the halfway mark and quarter marks. Because neither the toe section nor the tongue piece is perfectly round, it is impossible to find the midpoint by eye. You can't measure with a straight ruler, since you

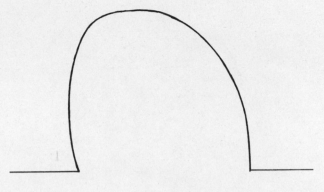

Step 1

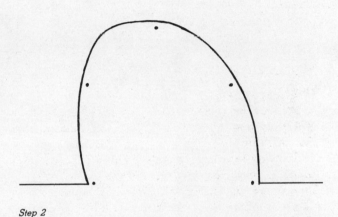

Step 2

Step 3

Determine the halfway point between each pair of holes. Usually this can be done with the eye.

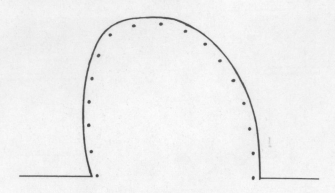

Step 4

Halve the spaces between the holes once again.

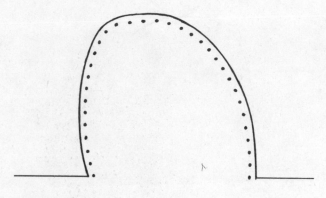

Step 5

Halve spaces once more.

are measuring a curve, and a tape is cumbersome and frequently not 100 percent accurate.

Use thread to find these half and quarter marks. Simply take a piece of thread or string and carefully trace it around the outside of the leather from the ball line to the ball line. Snip it off exactly, then fold it in half, lay it along the outside of the leather again, and you'll have the midpoint. Mark the leather about 1/8 inch in from the edge with small pen dots. Be careful of pen marks if your leather is light—they'll show. Now fold the string in half again to get your quarter points. These are your first two divisions. After that it is best to divide simply by using your eye. Keep dividing the areas in half five times.

Now repeat the procedure on the tongue piece.

Don't get lazy and try to lay the tongue over the toe part and mark it—it doesn't work. It takes more time and you get lots of errors. Measure and mark all four pieces individually, and everything will be perfect.

Gluing the Sole to the Bottom

Your first step in actually assembling the pieces of the moccasin is to glue the sole (or midsole, then sole) to the bottom, whichever side of the leather you have selected as the outside.

Your only problem will be positioning the sole properly on the bottom, so you can establish the area within which to spread the glue. You have to refer back to your pattern and retrace the measurements you made when you designed the bottom pattern. On the bottom you measured out from the sole 1½ inches to establish the perimeters of the toe area. Now you must measure 1½ inches in from the "corners" of the ball line on either side, make small marks, and line your sole up between the two marks. Around the toe the bottom was designed to be 1 inch longer than the outline of the sole pattern. Make a mark on the leather 1 inch in from the edge at the toe and line your sole up with this mark. The sole should now rest on the bottom 1 inch back from the edge of the leather at the toe and 1½ inches in from either side at the ball. The heel should be centered between the two notches or **V**'s on the heel of the bottom, and the whole thing should look exactly like the pattern.

Draw around the sole with a pen or awl, using the actual sole for this and not the paper pattern.

If you used the grain side of the hide on the outside of the moccasin, the leather will be smooth. Glue does not make a strong bond with a smooth surface unless you sand it or roughen it before applying the glue. Take some heavy-grit sandpaper and sand the leather within the pen line. Sand particularly well around the edges of the line, where the edge of the sole will be, since this outer edge is the area of greatest strain. If you are using galosh rubber as soling, it must be thoroughly sanded too, so that all the smooth, glossy look of the rubber is gone. Otherwise it will not hold.

Remember, if you will be using a midsole, don't start to spread the glue until 1/4 inch in from the edge. This will mean it won't be attached to the leather around the outer edges and the sole and midsole will be able to lie flat while the moccasin curves around your foot.

After the leather has been sanded, apply the glue evenly to both the bottom and the sole and wait until they are dry to the touch before putting them together (see pages 16–17).

When you put them together, don't forget that once the surfaces have made contact with each other they will be difficult to separate and trying to separate them will stretch both out of shape, so be careful.

Hover the sole over the bottom until the sole looks to you to be directly over the lines you have marked. Then set the heel in position and follow one edge around to the toe. Obviously, if you position one side of the sole carefully in place, the other will fall naturally where it belongs.

Once both soles are in position, hammer them all around the edges.

If you are using midsoles, it is now the time to sew them on. Look at the illustration (right) to see how all of this looks.

Setting the Inner Lining in the Moccasin

When you set the sole you hammered around the edges to make sure the sole was well in place, didn't you? Well! If you turn the moccasin to the inside where the lining will go, you will notice a dandy outline of the sole in the suede. Conveniently, your inner lining can be glued to this outline of the sole, since they are the same size. All you do is apply a thin—about ½ inch wide—rim of glue around the sole outline on the inside and on the bottom (suede side) of the inner lining, let them dry, then place the padding on the bottom and glue the inner lining to the moccasin bottom with the padding between the layers. You should have about ¼ inch of rim to glue to, which is generally plenty. Since we don't sew this down, we depend on the glue to hold it in position. The bond made by the two suede sides is the strongest possible bond and will generally hold, particularly when used as it is here, since you have constant weight on it. When you glue the lining to the bottom, just be careful to follow the outline and not have any padding sticking out.

SEWING

You have reached the big time now and are ready to sew. It does take some practice to get it nice and professional, and the process is difficult to describe, so bear with me.

You will need a needle and some thread. Use a blunt-ended harness needle, number 000. A lacing needle would probably not be strong enough (see page 21). The thread should be nylon and heavy.

It is hard to know how much thread the job will require and it is important to be aware of what an enormous frustration it is to run out of thread in the middle of sewing. (Actually, it is running out of thread two or three stitches before the finish that is the real frustration.) If you measure around the perimeter of the toe end of the bottom at least five times, this will give you plenty of thread. A quicker way is to use as much thread as the full stretch of your arms will give you.

Your sitting position is important. You should sit on a stool or a straight-backed chair so that you can get your arms and hands into a position where they exert the most strength. You should also be able to cross your legs so that you can have a working surface.

Sewing the Moccasin Bottom to the Tongue

Now, begin. You will no doubt have noticed that the bottom is quite a bit bigger than the tongue. Since these are the two pieces you will be sewing together, it should be apparent that you will have to gather up the extra material on the bottom to fit it around the tongue. It is necessary to get a gather on each stitch if the moccasin is to be neatly sewn and professional looking. Even if you have never sewn so much as a button, don't let this faze you. You will be using a simple cross-stitch which is very easy to do. It will be hard on your hands—if it isn't hard on your hands, you are probably not pulling the thread tightly enough or maintaining enough tension with your other hand.

Perhaps you are wondering why we use this method to sew—or lace—up the toe of the moccasin. You have no doubt seen dozens of commercial loafers and moccasins that claim to be handsewn and are sewn in a completely different manner. These are really sewn by hand. However, the makers use a last. It is a totally different method and involves a lot of equipment I don't feel is worthwhile. I have tried stitching moccasins the same way commercial manufacturers do, but unless you use a last to hold the moccasin in shape—they tack the leather to the last before they sew—it just isn't possible.

It is natural to stitch from the right side of the moccasin to the left if you are right-handed. Do whatever comes naturally, of course. Begin by putting a double knot at the end of the thread, or a knot large enough so it won't pull through the hole. Sometimes the thread is too lightweight and you will just have to tie a tight square knot to get the two pieces of leather joined.

Remember, and this is very important, *always have the knots on the outside of the leather.* All knots on any footwear should always be on the outside of the leather. They should be visible. Yes, I quite agree they are ugly; however, the appearance is unimportant when you compare it to a lump of thread constantly digging into your foot. It will not only rapidly drive you crazy, it will also create bad blisters and corns and foot problems. So you will just have to reconcile yourself to the idea that the knot will be visible.

When you have made your knot, leave a 2-inch "tail" at the end of the thread so that you can tie it off when you finish. You will finish sewing in the same spot where you began.

Put the needle through the first two holes from the outside of the bottom piece, pull the thread through to the knot, and then bring the thread over and go through the same holes again in the same direction. This holds the two pieces of leather firmly in position. Draw the thread very tight. Very, very tight. Leather stretches and generally nylon thread does too, so it is quite important to get a very tight stitch if the moccasin is to take a good shape. A tight stitch also helps to keep out dust, water, and pebbles. Now to start sewing.

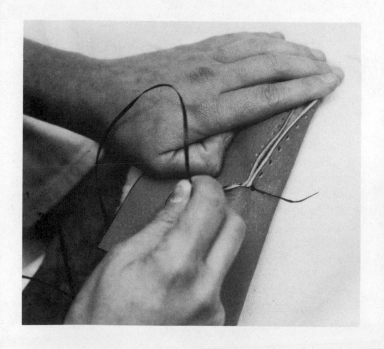
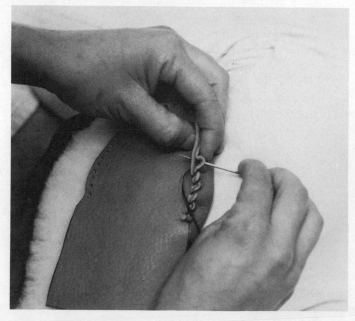

Put the needle through the next set of holes—that is, from hole 2 in the moccasin bottom to hole 2 in the tongue. Your stitch will cross over the leather. This is called a cross-stitch. At this point, holding tightly with your left hand, you will create the gather or pucker in the bottom so that the holes are opposite each other. If after taking the stitch there isn't an obvious pucker, use your needle and make one. This gathering must be done all the way along or you will end up with a big mass at the end of the stitching. Continue in this manner until you have reached the final set of holes on the left side (holes 33). Go through this set of holes two or three times to secure them and all the other stitches in position. Your left hand should feel quite cramped if you have been sewing the moccasin tight and close. You can take a coffee break and think that the worst is over.

To return. Now, you could go back, using the exact same cross-stitch you used going over. However, there is a minor variation that makes a better-looking and, oddly enough, a better-fitting finished product.

This time, going back, instead of stitching from hole 33 to 33, 32 to 32, and so on, go through hole 32 on the moccasin bottom (outside) and then back to hole 33 on the tongue. Pull the thread tight. Now go through hole 31 on the bottom and 32 on the tongue. Continue along in this manner back to the beginning. You can always see that you are going properly by checking the holes you just went through. At times it may look as if you have erred, but it may only appear that way because the direc-

tion of the sewing changes as you go around corners and so forth. Remember to place your thread in position over the pucker and make sure that the pucker is there. Compare your work with the photos. If it looks more or less similar, carry on. This stitching takes practice, so don't be disappointed if your first moccasin doesn't look like a professional job—you are not a pro yet.

To tie off the thread, get hold of the tail you left at the end of your original knot and use what is known as a half-hitch in sailing. You loop the loose end of the thread under the standing thread and up through the loop that forms. Pull this until the loop is tight under the knot. Then do another half-hitch the same way. Clip off the thread, leaving about ¼ inch at the ends. A knot in nylon thread can unravel. To prevent this, singe the ends of the thread so that they and part of the knot melt or congeal into one lumpy mass. It will never come undone.

You are finished. Try it on and see how it feels and fits. It should feel just super. If the toe of the moccasin looks rather bumpy and uneven, take the handle of a hammer and jam it around the inside of the toe. This should stretch it and shape it.

At this point the moccasin should feel just a wee bit tight, if you have followed directions so far and been careful. I assume that the leather will stretch as you wear it and that the padding will pack down and add more room. The moccasins are perfect if they are tight. If they are not, you can do one of two things. Carry on and worry about it later, if at all. Or you can flip ahead a few pages and check directions on how to fix things to perfect your fit.

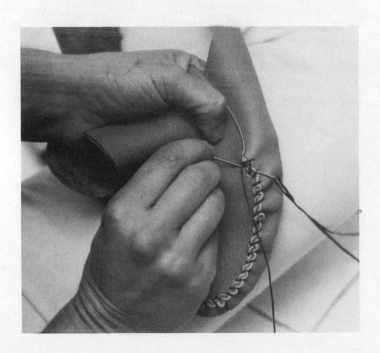
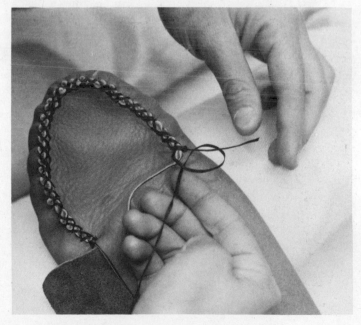

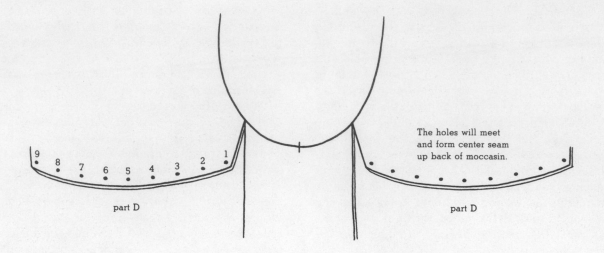

9 8 7 6 5 4 3 2 1

part D

The holes will meet
and form center seam
up back of moccasin.

part D

Sewing the Heel

There are two sewing steps involved in finishing up the heel section of the moccasin. First, you must sew —or lace—the two sides of the heel (parts D) together so that they form a seam at the center. Second, you must sew, with a stitching awl, the tab to the back, covering the seam.

SEWING THE BACK TOGETHER. I use the lacing method to sew the two sides together because this creates a seam that is smoothly butted. One edge of the leather meets the other edge without an overlap or a ridge of any kind and is flat on both the inside and the outside.

In order to do this you must punch some holes in both sides of the 3-inch heel sections. It doesn't really make a big difference how many holes you use, as long as you have an equal number on each side. I generally use nine holes because it involves a fast, three-step division and the holes are close enough together to make a good, tight stitch.

After punching the holes, cut off a piece of thread about 18 to 24 inches long. This might give you some excess thread, but it is much easier if you have too much than too little. Make a double knot the same way you did before, thread the needle, sit down, and begin.

The stitch is merely a cross-stitch. Simple. Start at the bottom, where the heel will touch the ground and sew through the first set of holes (hole 1 and hole 1), pulling the knot to the edge of the leather. Keep the knot on the outside so that it won't rub your foot. Now go through the same set of holes again so that the two sides are very tightly joined.

You want them edge to edge. I generally sew with my left hand inside the moccasin, so I can shape the curve as I sew and keep the edges from overlapping or from forming a ridge.

Now, go through the second set of holes, from the same side you started on. Pull tight and go through the second set once again. In other words, go through each set of holes twice, pulling the thread very tightly, until you reach the top set of holes, number 9. Sew set 9 three times to make absolutely certain that they are together and will stay together.

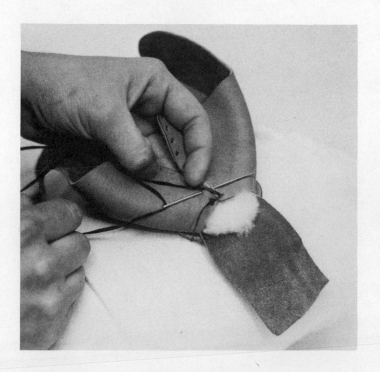

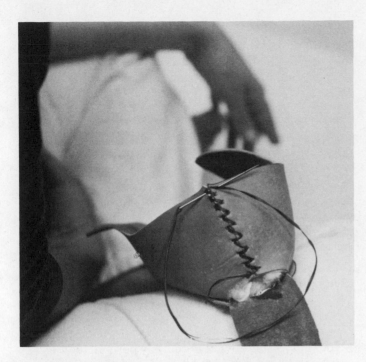

little bit back in the notches so that the sides touch at the heel.

Once you have reached holes 1 again, tie the knot in two half-hitches and clip off the thread. You don't need to singe it, since the entire seam will be covered by the tab.

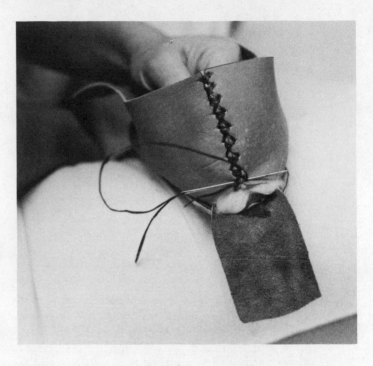

Now sew back down toward the knot. Going in this direction you need only go through each set of holes once. Go through twice on the way up to ensure that the leather stays in place and that the holes stay opposite each other. You don't want them to slip.

When you made the heel of the moccasin pattern you tapered the leather at the top and bottom of the two sides. This curved the two 1-inch edges so that you might have trouble bringing them together. If you cannot stretch them together, clip the leather a

SEWING THE TAB TO THE BACK.   It is just that simple: sew the tab to the back. First, you must glue the tab into place. Put the moccasin on or hold it stiff. Hold the tab in position, draw or score around the edges, put glue on both pieces, and wait until the glue is dry before putting the pieces of leather together. If you plan to make a top to add to the moccasin, your tab should be about ½ inch shorter than the height of the moccasin at the back. The top overlaps the heel by ½ inch and ideally should meet the tab so that they can be sewn together as one with a V stitch rather than a straight one. Whether or not you plan to use a top, the tab should be sewn on with the stitching awl. (Check pages 20–1 on using the stitching awl if you are at all confused.)

At this point you may want to get creative and design a more interesting tab than the straight one shown in most of the photos.

If you allotted the extra material on your pattern, your tab will be narrow at the bottom near the heel and very wide at the top. You can cut it down to any number of different shapes. Whatever shape you decide upon, don't make it any narrower at the bottom: you must have this width to cover the gaping hole down there.

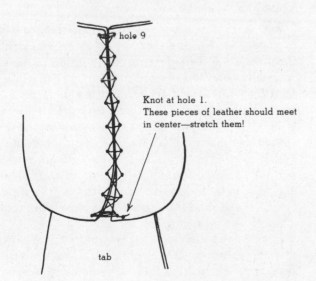

hole 9

Knot at hole 1.
These pieces of leather should meet in center—stretch them!

tab

FINISHING THE MOCCASIN

Except for the lace holes, your moccasins are finished. If you are satisfied with what you have now and want to wear them, pop in the lace holes and start hopping around. This is your basic moccasin, and this method of patternmaking will be used for nearly any moccasin you make unless you use one of the modifications discussed below for making specific types of moccasins. Or you may want to add a flap or a piece of reinforcement or any of the other decorations shown. Or maybe you will make a top to turn the moccasin into a boot (see pages 77–83).

Placing the Lace Holes

Put the moccasins on your feet. The pointed sections of leather that come up over your instep will either overlap or touch, depending on how big your foot is. To finish the moccasins, round off these points, cutting them down so that they end at least ½ inch apart. They will stretch that much. Now pull the two sides together and see where the pulling does the most good—where it eliminates the inevitable bag. Put marks for the top holes for the laces at that point. Put another set of marks about an inch back toward the heel from the first set. Punch the holes and put in your laces.

The size hole you punch depends, of course, on the size laces you plan to use. Most people select leather thongs because they are strong and long-

lasting. However, they do come untied easily and they are bulky. Use what you think looks best; it can change the look of the moccasin.

Reinforcement Pieces

These are essentially a matter of the limits of your imagination. Their purpose is to reinforce around the lace holes and the top edges of the moccasin. Use your moccasin as a pattern to design the reinforcement piece, then cut it out and glue it on. Stitch it on, using any straight or intricate stitch you can think of. It takes a lot of thinking sometimes to get your idea, but sooner or later you will come up with designs far more interesting than I can tell you about.

WHAT WENT WRONG?

If your moccasins are not absolutely perfect, please don't get discouraged or despondent and reupholster your couch with the rest of your hide, or let the dog sleep on your new sheepskin or destroy the moccasins. Although moccasins are the most difficult footwear to make perfectly from scratch, they have the saving grace of being the easiest to alter so that they are perfect. So relax, read through this catalog of suggestions, find your problem and the solution, and correct the problem. It is that simple.

Moccasins can come out being either too small or too big or just right, of course. If they are too small, you don't have quite as many options as if they are too large, so I'll run through this matter quickly.

Your Moccasins Are Too Small

I have never put on a newly made pair of moccasins or shoes that I didn't think I had made too small. Only once had I really goofed; every other time it was simply a matter of wearing them for a few hours until they had stretched out and the padding had packed down and conformed to my foot. If the leather you used was thick or not super-soft or was sheepskin, this may take a few days of gradual breaking in. It is very rare that they do not stretch out and become perfect, given the chance. They may stretch to the point of being too big, in which case you can read the suggestions for cutting them down in the following section.

If you used a soling that was stiffer or heavier than the galosh or dance rubber, it may be offering resistance and making them feel too tight. You can always remove the heavy sole and put on a lighter weight one. Flexibility in a shoe or moccasin is directly related to the thickness of the soling. Thin dance rubber moves exactly with your foot. The heavier soling stays down and does not move up when you flex your toes, so you need toe room inside for the toes to move around in. Thus, if you plan to use 24-iron crepe, for example, you should also add extra length to the foot pattern.

Some people simply have very large, muscular feet and the standard measurements are too small. This is rare. If you conclude this is your problem, find a friend with feet smaller than yours and give this pair away. On your next pair, expand the measurements. Measure your foot at the ball line and the toe and heel. Compare these measurements with those of your pattern, including the toe piece. The pattern shouldn't be any smaller than your foot measurements and not much more than ¼ inch larger. If the pattern and your foot don't correspond with each other, expand the measurements to 1¾ inches at the ball line, 1⅛ inches or 1¼ inches at the toe, and 3½ inches at the heel.

Another cause of trouble could be that you made a poor foot drawing. You probably did not hold the pen perpendicular to the foot, but angled it in such a way that the drawing is much smaller than your foot. If this is the reason the finished products are too small, there is no recourse other than to find a friend with a smaller foot and give the moccasins as a Christmas gift.

Your Moccasins Are Too Large

Whether you have made them that way or they have simply stretched out and you feel they are too sloppy, the alteration process is the same. If they are too large initially, there could be several causes.

Your foot drawing was probably inaccurate or you used a thick pen or you didn't follow the lines carefully enough when you cut out your pattern. Perhaps your sewing is weak or loose or the leather is very, very stretchy and stretched even as you worked with it. Perhaps the padding is not thick enough, in which case you can pull out the lining and change the padding and reglue the lining back in. Or some people just have a smaller foot than the standard measurements.

Obviously you will want to cut the moccasins down to make them smaller and better fitting. You can cut them down either at the heel or the toe or both. Cutting the moccasins down at the heel is easier and works well, but usually the basic problem is not at the heel but at the toe.

Try the moccasin on before you sew the heel backs together. If it feels very much too large—the front laces will tighten them up considerably—cut the **V** cuts deeper at the heel (angle **Y**). This will enlarge the back parts and shorten the moccasin, driving your foot forward. Cut the excess off one or both sides at the back, punch new holes, and sew the back up. This will make the tab a bit longer and the sole protrude farther. Cut off the excess tab but leave the soling. It protects the leather from heel dragging.

This is a really good method of making the moccasin smaller once it is well under way. It is a good idea to have a customer come in for a fitting of the moccasin before you sew the heel. If it fits well, the customer is happy and can't wait for delivery. If it is too large, the moccasins can be cut down right there and the customer is still happy because of that personal attention.

To tighten the moccasin at the toe section, you have the option of trimming away excess from the tongue piece or the bottom piece. Be sure to note where the moccasin is too big. Generally it is too long, not too wide. Don't cut away width unless you know it is necessary.

When you cut the toe down, simply remove the sewing, carefully cut away the holes and the material you feel unnecessary, punch new holes, and resew them. It makes a world of difference.

If you cut down the tongue piece, just cut away the existing holes in the toe area, not necessarily around the ball line. This will shorten the toe by about ³⁄₁₆ inch, which is generally more than adequate. The result will be a more baggy- and gathered-looking moccasin, because you are now actually gathering much more material around a smaller tongue piece. Many people love this look; they feel it looks more Indian.

If you cut down the bottom piece, simply cut away the existing holes around the toe area. This eliminates excess, which is cumbersome and annoying. It avoids the bagging problem you get with the tongue piece solution and looks and feels, I think, much better.

Generally the moccasins are noticeably too large on feet smaller than standard measurements: women size 7 and under, jockeys, kids, and teenagers. Since it is much easier to redesign the pattern than it is to worry about it after things are finished, measure the thickness of the foot (toe height and heel height) and use the measurements of the foot.

Usually the only modification necessary is to make the toe area of the bottom piece smaller. Instead of 1 inch around the big to little toe area, use ¾ or ⅞ inch. It seems like a minuscule change, but makes a tremendous difference in fit for smaller feet, and is usually all that is necessary. I've never used less than ¾ inch, even for a year-old child.

You can lower the height of the heel section from 3 inches to 2¾ inches or 2½ inches—on adults never lower.

You can decrease the 1½-inch ball-line measurement to 1⅜ or 1¼ inches but you should be very careful because small feet usually have high arches and are thick in the middle, then thin out rapidly at the toes.

Don't decrease these measurements if you are using a thicker than galosh rubber soling.

MOCCASIN VARIATIONS

Cutting the Moccasin Down

If you don't like the feel or look of the moccasin around your ankles, you can cut away that material so that it undercuts the ankle with a swoop or straight line, like the very traditional moccasins. Just plan it out before you cut, and cut as smoothly as you can. There are no real rules here—just don't cut the moccasin too low, and don't lower it at the back.

Using a Midsole

For a number of reasons you may want to use a midsole on your moccasins. A midsole is what the name implies: a sole or a very thin piece of leather that goes between the outer sole and the moccasin bottom. You'll use it when the leather is too oily to bond well with the sole or when the soling is too stiff to curve with the moccasin bottom. Therefore, you'll sew the midsole onto the moccasin bottom— before you put in padding—and glue the outer sole to the midsole. Then the outer sole will not come off. You can't sew through solings by hand. Even if you could, you shouldn't, because the stitches would be exposed to the walking surface, you'd soon walk through the thread, and the sole would pull off. Thus you use a midsole. Good commercial loafers are made with this midsole, which makes the moccasin resolable. Otherwise it is good only until you've walked through the stitches.

Hand stitching takes time, but it is well worth the effort, since you'll never have problems with the sole coming off. The moccasin is designed to curve from the bottom around your foot. Solings (other than those made of galosh rubber) are designed to lie flat. The two are incompatible. A midsole sewn to the bottom solves this problem and enables you to use any thickness or weight of soling you select.

Glue the midsole to the moccasin bottom, leaving an unglued outer rim of ¼ inch. Then sew on the midsole about ¼ inch in from the edge. This means the outer ¼ inch of midsole is in no way connected to the moccasin bottom, although it is under your foot. When you wear it, the bottom leather is free to curve around your foot and the sole is free to lie flat. It works out very well, and if you're putting eight hours into a pair of high sheepskin moccasins, for example, another hour isn't going to add much.

It doesn't seem to make any difference what weight or thickness or type of leather you use for the midsole. Glue the grain side to the bottom so the suede side will glue to the sole and create a strong bond.

Children's Moccasins

Making children's moccasins is just a matter of measuring the foot and using these measurements to develop the pattern. The ball line doesn't go back the full ⅝ inch, but about ⅜ or ¼ inch on very small toddlers. Much depends on the size of the child.

The thick, 1-inch padding is too much for a child's moccasin. Children's feet don't need it, they don't have the weight to pack it down, and it is terribly difficult to calculate how much padding will take up how much space. Leave it out and substitute a thin inner lining of sheepskin—not glued in place—to make their feet happy.

Don't allow growing room. Make the pattern to the foot drawing, and the leather will stretch and provide growing room.

At the ball line start with a measurement of no less than 1½ inches and reduce this around the toe area to no less than ¾ inch, for even the smallest child. Generally the tongue piece should not be reduced by much less than ⅛ inch, and the total of

the tongue piece plus the bottom measurement should be at least ½ inch larger than the measurement of the foot around the ball. Small children do not have the foot muscles to jam their feet into the moccasin, and you have to provide extra room just to get the foot in and get the shoe laced.

At the heel the backs should measure what the child's foot measures from the floor to the bend at the heel, generally about 2¼ inches.

Slippers

People like slippers to be designed to do what they say they do: slip on. It has taken years to figure out a design and create moccasins that don't instantly break down, get slovenly, and fall off the foot with each step. Part of the secret of preventing this is placing the ball line way behind (⅝ to ¾ inch) the ball, so that the moccasin stays on the foot when laced.

If you want the reverse of this—shoes you can slip on and off—you put the ball line at the ball of the foot. Then you've designed something that will be no tighter than the ball, or widest part, of the foot, and thus it comes off easily.

The low shape undercuts the ankles, swooping down from the lace area, under the ankles, and up to the heel. This can be cut out of the moccasin when finished or be designed into your pattern before you begin. Just be sure to provide enough material to lace over the instep.

There is a finishing "welt" around the top edge of the moccasin. It is made by using a straight strip of leather the width of a ruler, about 1¼ inches, and the length of the distance around the top edge. Glue half the strip inside the moccasin and half outside, hammer around to pack down the welt, particularly at the corners, and stitch it on. Naturally you can also make this design with the ball line in the usual place so that it stays on.

Flap Design

This popular—and easy—low moccasin is an authentic Indian design. Make the usual moccasin pattern with one variation. The extension at the ball line for extra leather (generally 2 inches over the instep) should be made only 1 inch beyond the 1½-inch mark. The 1 inch should extend to the regular heel height of 3 inches.

The flap pattern provides a starting point for you to design your own. There is a 1-inch portion which is simply glued to the inside of the moccasin, with the flap part outside. Don't bother to sew it on—it receives no stress and glue will hold quite well enough. Start at this point in your patternmaking and measure the moccasin from the ball line around the heel to the ball line. This is the distance of your 1-inch folded piece. The flap portion on the outside curves to a point about 1 or 1¼ inches beyond the ball-line point, toward the toe. It is an ideal style for a short foot, since it gives the illusion of length. There is a point in the back and near the middle that nearly hits the ground. When you punch your lace holes, put them through the leather of the moccasin, not through the flap.

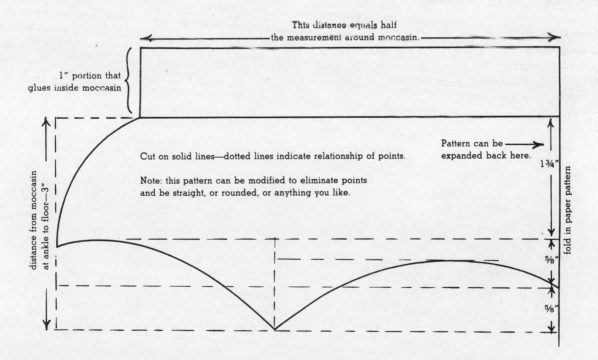

This distance equals half the measurement around moccasin.

1" portion that glues inside moccasin

distance from moccasin at ankle to floor—3"

Cut on solid lines—dotted lines indicate relationship of points.

Note: this pattern can be modified to eliminate points and be straight, or rounded, or anything you like.

Pattern can be expanded back here.

1¾"

fold in paper pattern

⅝"

⅝"

This flap idea can be very effective if made into a straight piece of material surrounding the moccasin or by adding curves or whatever strikes your imagination.

Sheepskin Moccasins

No question about it, sheepskin moccasins will be your most popular moccasin, and you should promise yourself the treat immediately. They look warm and cozy, they *are* warm and cozy, they feel great, and there just aren't enough nice things to say about them. You can always get a good fit with sheepskin —it fills every curve of the foot whether you designed the pattern properly or not.

The only problem is that few people end up wearing these moccasins just padding around the house as they planned. The moccasins are so comfortable that sooner or later you wear them outside, every day, in subzero temperatures or just chilly weather. Sheepskin is a very weak leather. It cannot stand this sort of wear, and it tears very easily. Although the wool will last forever, the hide to which it is attached is tender and will give if you stitched it too tight, or after two or three years it will weaken and tear. The solution to this is always to cover any sheepskin moccasin you make with an outer layer or shell of leather—thin garment cow or deer if you feel flush, or regular 4- to 6-ounce cow if the moccasins are to be after-ski, high-boot-top models that you know will get lots of wear. And always put a sole on a sheepskin moccasin.

Sheepskin moccasins can be made in many forms, ranging from an extra inner lining you cut to slip into a regular leather moccasin to the high, lined snow or ski boot. Wool either ½ inch or ¾ inch thick can be used. The ½ inch is ideal for baby moccasins or lightweight moccasins. The ¾ inch makes a heavier, warmer, more cushioned mocca-

sin, and its only disadvantage is that when first made the moccasins are extremely tight with an extra ¾ inch of wool on the top, bottom, and sides and there isn't much room for the foot. If you use sheepskin with wool ¾ inch thick, you have to be prepared to jam your foot in and pack down the wool.

PATTERN MODIFICATIONS. These are to allow for the bulk of sheepskin. Actually there are very few changes you must make in your pattern. Do the bottom exactly as usual; don't deviate on the standard measurements, even for small feet. A minor change in the tongue piece is that it should be narrowed by only ⅛ inch instead of ⅜ inch. That is the only change necessary for the bottoms of sheepskin moccasins. The changes in making a top are greater (see Boots, page 80) because the leg does not put the pressure on the wool that the foot does and the wool doesn't pack down.

Low moccasins. The easiest style to make is obviously the low, basic model shaped to cover your ankles or cut beneath them. Sheepskin moccasins are extremely bulky. They make your foot look fat. Very few people are vain about this when it's cold, but if you are, you can make a low model using leather with sheepskin on the bottom as the inner lining and as a lining for the tongue. This eliminates the wool on the side of the foot, which makes it look so bulky, and it doesn't eliminate much warmth.

Sheepskin is very expensive. There is a lot of waste because the skin is so small and the smaller a skin or hide is the less of it you are able to use. When you lay out your pattern take the time to figure the very best way to use the area you have. One skin will give you about two pairs of low moccasins or one pair of high, boot-type moccasins. Plan carefully: double-check that you've flipped the patterns, and make sure there is wool beneath the parts of the skin you are using. Around the leg areas of the skin there is no wool and you must be careful to avoid these places.

High moccasins. These take ten hours to make. They are really two pairs of moccasins glued together, one inside the other, and should have a midsole with a thin 9-iron outer sole. You must design your entire moccasin from the start so you have all the pieces to lay out on the skin and can determine the best way to use it. You don't have to cut your top at this time—just plan it. Cut out all the sheepskin pieces, bottom pieces and high tongue piece. Then cut out leather bottom pieces and a short leather tongue piece that will cover the foot as high as the instep. Sew the midsole to the bottom pieces of leather. Glue on the sole. Then glue the two together. This takes patience: the glue on your hands gets covered with the loose fuzz of the wool and it's very messy. Cut off the tab portion on the sheepskin bottom, which is only excess bulk and serves no purpose. Lacing up the tongue-toe area takes a lot of strength because there is so much material. Sew up the backs and try the moccasins on. They should be tight. Then try on your paper top pattern, cut it out of sheepskin, and design the reinforcement pieces you plan to use. The lace area should definitely be reinforced, because the skin is so fragile.

Sewing with your stitcher through the sheepskin is annoying because you can't see the loop on the needle. Attach a safety pin to the end of the "bobbin" thread to help you when you're feeling for the loop inside the wool.

These moccasins are super, and a labor of love.

Moccasin Work Boots

A superior heavy-duty moccasin for working, hiking, or any active situation is easily created by using two layers of 4-ounce leather. Don't use latigo: it isn't nearly as durable or strong as two layers bonded together, and it doesn't gather or glue well.

Because of the added bulk, plus the toe room you will need for strenuous work, you'll have to expand your measurements slightly—sole pattern: increase the length in the toe area by about 1/8 inch; bottom: no change; tongue: in making the tongue pattern from the sole pattern, decrease the pattern by only 1/8 inch, not 3/8 inch.

Each moccasin is basically two moccasins— bottom, tongue, and top—glued together. Use a strong midsole and sew it to the outer moccasin before gluing it to the inner one. Sandwich the padding between the two layers with the inner moccasin acting as the inner lining. Glue the two moccasins suede side to suede side, so that the grain is next to your foot. Spread glue all over both surfaces, and carefully match the pieces together. The inner layer of the tongue piece need not extend all the way up the ankle; it just has to go over the toe area for protection.

When you glue the top to the moccasin, glue the outer layer to the outside of the moccasin and the inner layer to the inside. Keep the moccasin between the two layers of the top so it doesn't make a ridge to rub your foot.

You can use any soling you select for this heavy moccasin, including Vibram. Should you use this,

select the brand with the heel preattached to the sole so that you don't have to nail it on.

The top can, of course, be any size or height you desire. A low top that covers the ankle, but does not bind it or restrict it, is probably the best.

On this model, or in fact on any moccasin or shoe, you can punch small holes with your stitcher around the bottom edge to permit air to circulate.

Moccasins Using Needlepoint and Other Media

If you do needlepoint or embroider or weave you probably want to put some of your work into a moccasin. It can easily be done, although the finishing part might give you some pause. I don't know enough about the ins and outs of these crafts to tell you everything you need to know, but I'll give you some pointers.

Embroidery—and beadwork—can be done directly onto some thin, weak types of leather like sheepskin (without the wool it is a very thin, delicate leather) or chamois. You can make a pattern for the beadwork using your moccasin tongue or the sides of the moccasin and glue it onto the leather you are using for your moccasin. You could certainly glue or sew a piece of fabric, as long as it isn't too stiff, to a moccasin, particularly a sheepskin one.

Needlepoint presents problems only because it is so stiff and you must use leather under the canvas to protect your foot. The easy way is to make your needlepoint design the exact (as exact as is possible) size of the tongue piece, and bind off the edges. Prepunch the holes in the leather tongue piece, glue the needlepoint to the leather, and sew up the toe area, just pushing the needle through the needlepoint wherever it happens to come up. Keep in mind that this makes a rather stiff toe area, without much gathering.

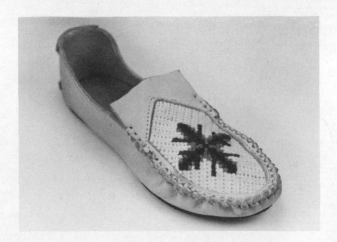

A more involved method, which looks more finished, is to measure in on the tongue pattern ¼ inch and use this inner portion as the needlepoint design area. Do the same thing for any side areas, if you wish, being careful not to get your design into the gathered part of the bottom. The ¼-inch border will be leather. When you finish your design, make a plastic or acetate template to cover the perimeter of the design, put this template over the moccasin leather tongue piece, and cut away any leather that would be under the template. This should leave an enormous hole in your leather tongue piece (or side piece) and the needlepoint design should fit right in. Then you can sew or simply glue the canvas to the leather with a machine. Be careful not to get glue on the needlework. To finish, glue a tongue piece of leather (thin deerskin, for example) or sheepskin under the needlepoint to protect the foot, then punch your holes and finish as usual. This second method is more involved, but makes a much more finished, less bulky item. In either case it's a labor of love.

REPAIRING YOUR MOCCASINS

You made your moccasins; you know every inch, every stitch, and every measurement in them. You made them; you can repair and restore them when they need it. Redo whatever is necessary, using the same procedures you used when you first made them. Restitch them, cutting them down if necessary, dye them to bring them back to life, polish them, and resole them.

Resoling might be your only problem. Just peel off the old sole, make a pattern from it, and put on a new one. If you are a heel dragger and have worn a hole in the back there, make a small tablike extension on the new sole that will curve up and cover the hole. Pop in a few stitches to hold it permanently in place.

Shoes

We have all been wearing shoes all our lives, yet few of us have any idea how they are made. I suspect that one reason for the popularity of handmade moccasins is that the avid do-it-yourselfer can easily see that a moccasin is a piece of leather that somehow wraps around the foot. Thus it is fairly simple to conceptualize the creation of one. A shoe, however, has lots of hidden parts, and its construction to most is unimaginable: something too difficult to attempt. Yet there is absolutely nothing difficult about making a shoe. It is, in fact, easier to make a shoe that fits perfectly than it is to make a moccasin that fits perfectly, and it takes less time! Once you understand what is involved in creating a shoe, you will wonder why no one has ever explained it before.

Because we—Jim—had no idea how a shoe was made, but we—he—wanted to make one, his mind was uncluttered by the traditions of shoemaking. After a lot of creative thinking and inventive experimentation, he has devised a shoemaking technique that is, as far as I know, unique.

All other shoemakers in all other times have always used what is known in the trade as a last. A last is traditionally a piece of wood shaped like a foot. The shoemaker uses this last to mold the leather around and build the shoe from the inside out. It is the same principle as the mannequin a dressmaker uses when the customer is not available for a fitting.

We have never used a last. We use the foot for a last and thus have freed ourselves and others to create shoes inexpensively and easily. It sounds so simple when we say we use the foot for a last that you are probably reading without even the blink of an eyelash. And yet our method is almost revolutionary. When we tell shoemakers or cobblers that we make shoes this way, they do not believe us and think we mean moccasins or sandals. When we tell them we do not use a last, they dismiss us and are not interested in listening because they do not believe it can be done. Well, despite that, I can confidently call myself a shoemaker because we have made hundreds of custom-made shoes and seen dozens of students leaping about in their own homemade, comfortable, well-fitted, and attractive shoes.

Of course, there are limitations to these methods.

Because the actual human foot is used to create the shape of the shoe, you must always have a welt or small ridge on the outside of the shoe. The leather is stretched and fitted over the foot and glued to the edge of the sole, rather than tucking it underneath the foot as in a commercially made shoe. Because of this limitation, plus the fact that you will not use expensive machinery, you cannot create delicate dancing and cocktail shoes or traditional men's business shoes. But you can create good, solid, comfortable shoes to work and play in and for your children to work and play in, shoes that will be durable and attractive and cost a great deal less than anything you are able to buy today.

HOW A SHOE IS MADE

In order to understand what you are about, it might be interesting to have a little background on traditional shoemaking methods and the use of a last.

The most famous and expensive custom-made shoe today is the Space shoe. This is an excellent, well-built shoe, and for people with serious foot problems, it is well worth the $150 or whatever is charged for each pair. Our side-opening style was derived from this famous orthopedic shoe. Manufacturers begin forming it by making plaster-of-Paris casts of the individual's feet. From these casts or negatives, a positive or exact replica of the feet is made. Then they carefully construct the shoes around the replicas or lasts. Few of us need such an elaborate reproduction of our feet in order to obtain a good fit. The technique described below is the next best thing to making a one-time casting of the foot. And it doesn't cost $150.

Commercial manufacturers also use lasts in the production of their shoes. The manufacturer is primarily creating a style, then creating a shoe that will fit. His goal is to make a sale; otherwise he will not stay in business. Staying in business these days means tremendous competition for the consumer dollar, and that means offering shoes in many many styles and colors. While you may be bewildered by the enormous selection, he is bewildered by what you will select and therefore creates a lot for you to choose among.

For a manufacturer to make a shoe, he must have

not only a last in the shape of the foot but also one in the style of the shoe being made. If he is offering a pointed-toe style the last must have a pointed toe. If he is creating a pointed-toe style in three different heel heights, he must have three different pointed-toe lasts for each of the heel heights.

To a manufacturer a set of lasts is an enormous investment. Consider that shoes generally run in ten half and full sizes and five widths, and it obviously means that he must have fifty sets of lasts for just one style. Lasts are made by special companies and are very expensive. At best a commercial last is only a reasonable facsimile of an average foot. If you have a foot that is not "average," you will have problems getting anything comfortable.

I have never tried to make a pair of lasts myself, but I did once try to cut out a pair of clogs for myself on a bandsaw. It was then that I came to understand why good custom makers charge more than $100 just to create the last. I was easily able to sculpt out a right clog that looked good and seemed comfortable. The problem came in trying to sculpt a left clog that was the exact opposite of the right one, but was still its mate. By the time they looked like a pair they were an inch smaller than my foot. I was only trying to make a clog that fit the bottom of my foot. A last must resemble the whole foot, with all its curves and rises at the instep. It is a very exacting job and probably explains why only in recent times—the last seventy-five years or so—shoes have been made specifically for the left or the right foot. Prior to that they were made on straight lasts and could be worn, at least initially, on either foot. I can only assume that the old-timers would have used our methods if they had had the materials and leathers available to them that we have today.

There are no hard-and-fast rules of shoemaking from this point of view. The two biggest challenges you will face will be in drawing a good foot pattern for the sole and in molding the leather well over your foot. The most important objective is getting a good fit. Everything else is flexible. I mention this because I can hear echoing in my memory student voices questioning every little thing. As we go along, I'll try to give a reason for each step so that you can understand its purpose and then make the decision about whether to do it or not. While the twenty or so processes involved in making the shoe may seem to be long and tedious, they all move along very rapidly and you can make a shoe in less than four hours. In a commercial shoe manufacturing plant there are more than 250 different processes, so our few seem quite simple indeed.

In order to make a shoe you must have a sole and an upper and some means of attaching one to the other. If you want a boot, you must add a top to the upper. You don't need a heel, but you can make a wedge if you want one. You don't need padding, but everyone always elects to have it. You don't have to have a hard, durable, thick sole; you can use a soft, flexible one if you prefer that kind. It is all a matter of your taste and the needs you have for that particular shoe.

We have essentially two basic designs or patterns for shoe uppers: the side-opening model, the front-opening model, and a variation, the front-opening model with the toe cap. All the varieties of shoes come from one of these designs. I will detail the creation of these basic designs in the coming sections and suggest changes, variations, improvements, and embellishments that you can make after you have tried one of the basic types. I know it is rewarding, fun, and easy, so let's get started.

Your shoes will be as comfortable as the care you put into them. You'll have a misfit only if you don't take the time to pay attention to detail. Shoes require your attention and thought all the way through their construction.

Keep in mind that a shoe is really two parts. Shoes —and sandals—can be thought of as having tops or uppers (the part that covers your foot) and lowers or bottoms (the part under the foot). Each part requires its own pattern and its own special attention to detail. The soles, once the pattern is made, have only to be cut out, then finished a bit so that the shoes look decent. The uppers frequently require refitting or minute alterations as you progress, and you cannot stop thinking until that last lace is tied and you are striding about.

While the uppers of shoes and sandals have no similarities, the method of constructing the soles is exactly the same in both. Much of the background and the procedures necessary for understanding and making sandals appears in this chapter on shoes. Whatever soling, heeling, or wedging you can put on a shoe, you can do the same on a sandal. The soles are finished in the same way. Whatever is unique to sandals appears in that chapter, but, for the sake of brevity, whenever a procedure or bit of information is the same for a sandal as for a shoe you will be asked to refer to this chapter.

There is no rigid order in making either type of footwear. The only rule is that you must have the bottoms cut and ready to attach to the cut and ready upper. After the parts have been attached, your attention then shifts between finishing work on the uppers and the bottoms, and it makes little difference which you do first or in what order, just so that everything gets done. We'll deal with the bottoms or sole part of the shoe first.

BOTTOMS

To make this bottom you'll need a sole pattern, which is derived from the foot drawing.

Making the Sole Pattern from the Foot Drawing

The sole pattern will determine the shape of the shoe. Make a new foot drawing (see pages 29–30), compare the feet, get a pencil, and draw. Take time and ponder over every little scratch you make—you'll have to look down at this shape you've created for a long time to come.

Essentially, the pattern shape is the shape of your foot, as are all the sole patterns—although they aren't all exactly alike. Examine the sample patterns provided in this section and compare them with those in other sections to get help in shaping the toe area. Here are some guidelines to remember as you draw around each area of the foot.

TOE AREA.   This is the trickiest area to shape well since there are so many configurations of toes. Of all footwear, shoes require the most toe room; you should allow about ¾ inch of space beyond the longest toe. It will probably look excessive to you, but this ¾ inch includes a ¼-inch allotment for the stitching or nailing line as well. You just can't inhibit toe movement. For some small women, size 6½ or less, ⅝ inch is probably adequate, at least for a lightweight shoe.

BALL AREA.   Leave at least ⅛ inch of room at the widest part of the foot, the ball area. Don't get vain and try to reduce this, or you'll walk to regret it.

When the lines at the toe and ball are connected, the result, particularly in wide-footed people, is often a shape that resembles a Ping-Pong paddle. If you aren't wild about this decidedly handmade shape, gently redraw the line to eliminate any big bulges. You can draw the line right on the side of the toes; they don't need extra room.

ARCH-INSTEP AREA.   The shoe should be fairly snug here. To make them snug, don't follow the outline of the arch area, but draw your sole-pattern line about ⅛ inch inside this line. This procedure is used in all the footwear in this book.

HEEL AREA.   After passing the anklebones, trace outside the drawing line at least ⅛ inch all the way

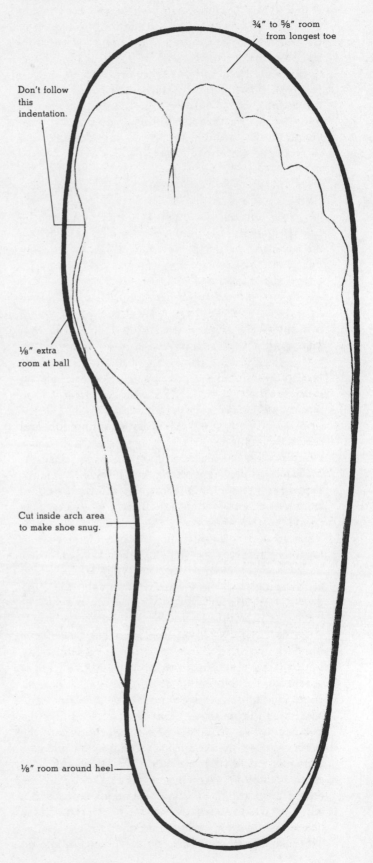

Shoe Sole Pattern

¾" to ⅝" room from longest toe

Don't follow this indentation.

⅛" extra room at ball

Cut inside arch area to make shoe snug.

⅛" room around heel

around the heel. Reshape the heel lines to make a rounded heel for the shoe. A well-fitted shoe is snug at the heel, encouraging the natural movement of up and down, not side to side. Shoes feel sloppy if the heel fits too loosely.

Drawing these patterns takes practice. When you feel you have a good pattern that follows all the guidelines, cut it out. Turn the completed pattern over. Without all the scribblings, you can see what shape you have and alter it if you need to. Be on the lookout for the hooked foot.

Making the Sole

The sole portion of either shoes or sandals can be constructed without a midsole and nailed, or with a midsole and nailed or sewn. You'll have to make decisions for both so it seems a good idea to describe the choices.

CONSTRUCTION WITHOUT A MIDSOLE. A shoe (or sandal) can easily be constructed with a leather sole nailed to the upper with some padding between the sole and some sort of liner. This method is your most basic form of construction and the one most frequently associated with handmade footwear. But it has several disadvantages: (1) You are limited to leather soling since rubber solings can't be nailed. (2) You have to nail because hand sewing through leather is a nasty business. (3) When you need to resole you'll have to remove the old sole, which in these shoes will be the entire bottom portion, and it is difficult to reassemble things so that they are again your old beloveds. Thus you are limited to the lifespan of the leather sole. (4) Every shoe looks alike. We used this method for a long time until everyone was so bored with the lack of variety we started developing alternative methods.

CONSTRUCTION WITH A MIDSOLE. The alternative method of construction is to use a midsole. This midsole is a "lost" (useless, because of the grain or whatever) piece of latigo or harness leather or even regular leather that is connected to the upper and separates it from the bottom or outer sole. It is between the two. You sew or nail the uppers to the midsole, then glue your outer soling to the midsole. This method has a few distinct advantages: (1) You have a choice of sewing or nailing. (2) You can select any soling or combination of solings you want. (3) Resoling is easy, since you can peel off the old soling without disturbing the upper portion. Thus the life of the item is indefinite, depending

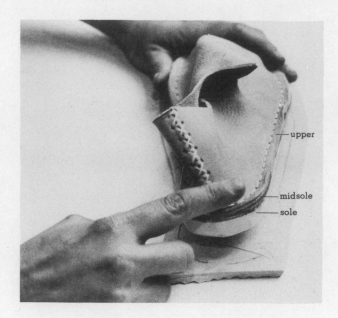

only on how long the uppers last. Very good ready-made shoes have this midsole, and it is frequently the primary difference between a popular, expensive shoe and its cheap imitation.

Sewing or Nailing On the Sole

The use of the midsole opens up the choice of sewing or nailing shoes and sandals.

SEWING THE SHOES. Most people elect the sewing method because the result looks so much more finished and refined—the shoe looks like a real, professionally made shoe. Women in particular consider a nailed shoe to look cloddy, cumbersome, ungainly, and out of place. It doesn't compliment even casual clothing.

You need fewer tools and equipment to sew shoes and can do the sewing anywhere you choose, in your living room or at the beach or even at the office during lunch hour. We have had virtually no bad fits with the sewn shoe because the foot can spread and stretch the leather over the stitching line. Sewing is more permanent and durable; you cannot pull out the individual stitches as you can nails, and nylon thread will stretch but not break under the extreme pressure an active foot can exert.

NAILING THE SHOES. Some like the unique, handmade look that nailing gives a shoe; it looks heavy, rugged, and masculine. It draws attention to your feet, particularly when the brass nails are still bright and untarnished. It is different and unusual and interesting. Nailing is faster than sewing (30 minutes versus 60), but you have the problem of needing an anvil, nails, and a hammer. It is unlikely that you will want to lug a 5-pound anvil to the beach or the office. Finally, nailing shoes requires an extra strip of narrow leather around the perimeter in order to distribute the pressure of the nails and ensure that the two parts will stay together. This welt, as it is called by the trade, confines the foot and sometimes the shoe is quite tight at first and difficult to break in.

These methods are fairly straightforward; you just have to make a choice before you begin. I have a strong preference for the midsole method with sewing.

Whichever method you select, the midsole or not, the padding and the inner lining will be sandwiched together on top of it to become what we will call the bottom, for lack of a more sophisticated trade term. The bottom will then be molded to the upper to become the single unit: the shoe.

Inner Linings, Midsoles, and Padding

For the lining (which will go next to your foot but inside the shoe) select a not especially pretty part of the soft hide, a piece that has stretch marks or is stretchy in itself. It's a good way to use up these undesirable sections, provided they don't have any ridges or lumps to irritate the foot.

For midsoles I prefer to use a piece of latigo or harness (belly) leather, around 7 ounces, because that weight is rigid but still easy to sew through. You can use a stiff portion of the soft hide; the stiffness merely helps hold the bottom shape until the molding is finished.

After selecting the various pieces of leather mentioned above, cut out the midsoles, using the paper sole pattern. Draw around it, flip it, and draw around it again. Careful cutting now will pay off for you later.

PADDING. See page 14. The leather sole should be cut out now if you've chosen the traditional single-sole method. If you're using the midsole method, don't cut out the final sole yet—you'll use the assembled shoe for the pattern, not the paper. Leather soling is hard to cut, so use a new blade and draw and cut from the wrong (inner) side so you'll have a line to follow when you glue.

Gluing the Bottoms

As usual when you use padding, put glue on only the outer ½-inch edge of each piece (see page 45). Glue the sueded side of the lining, since you want the grain side next to your foot. Glue the lining to the grain side of the midsole, because you want

the more absorbent, better-bonding side available for attaching to the outer sole. Wait until the glue has dried before pressing the pieces together.

Because the midsole is thin, the shape of the assembled pieces frequently looks distorted, bending and curving and rounding out on both sides. Don't be concerned. Once you attach the firm outer sole it will straighten out and be flat and normal.

The bottom is now ready for molding, but first make your uppers.

UPPERS

Patterns

I use two basic patterns for the tops or uppers of the shoe: a front opening and a side opening. These patterns and all modifications or style variations are one piece of leather with reinforcement and decorative pieces or tops added later. This method of using one piece is much easier to design, eliminates finicky measuring, and lends itself readily to our method of molding the leather. The more pieces you have (as in ready-made kits), the more sewing and work there is, with more seams to rub and irritate the foot, and the trickier it is to achieve a good fit.

The front-opening pattern should be used if you plan to make boots and add a top or if you simply want a more traditional type of shoe. You can make infinite variations on the opening of this model, thus changing the appearance around the ankles or instep. The one reproduced on page 74 is merely the one I use most frequently.

The side-opening style is unique and looks interesting. It has the advantage of taking the pressure of the laces and tongue off the sensitive top of the

Side Opening Pattern for Adult Shoes

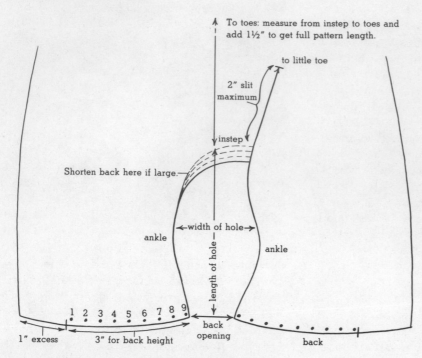

To toes: measure from instep to toes and add 1½″ to get full pattern length.

to little toe

2″ slit maximum

instep

Shorten back here if large.

width of hole

ankle

ankle

length of hole

1 2 3 4 5 6 7 8 9

1″ excess

3″ for back height

back opening

back

Length of hole = distance from heel tendon to bone over instep (where foot creases).

Length of hole + distance from instep to toes + 1½″ will determine *total* length of pattern. Connect total length with 4″ width marks at back for total pattern. Double-check with measurement from floor to floor over instep.

instep and foot and placing it on the side of the foot, where there is less strain. The opening is wide and allows the leather to come under the anklebones for maximum movement. This style is definitely recommended for people with foot problems or such high arches that they can't find shoes that don't pinch or hurt their insteps. It is extremely comfortable, very popular with our customers and students, and everyone seems to love it. Trying to make a boot from this pattern is not a good idea because of the unusual position of the lace opening.

Whichever basic pattern you select, it will be one piece with an opening at the back. This opening is sewn up to create a leather top or upper with a hole for your foot. These openings are essentially a one-size-fits-all. You will be perfectly safe in using these patterns for openings exactly as they appear, but if you measure and decide they need to be shortened, appropriate places for shortening are indicated. The openings are based on the measurement of your foot from the top of the instep where you want the shoe to stop to the point at your heel where it bends, about 2¾ inches from the floor. The back pieces are 4 inches: 3 inches for the height of the shoe (2¾ inches for actual height and ¼ for the seam) and 1 inch of excess needed for molding.

The leather is then stretched over the contours of the foot, glued to the edges of the sole, and the excess is cut away. Thus the only seams that finally remain are at that back opening.

Front Opening Pattern for Child's Shoes

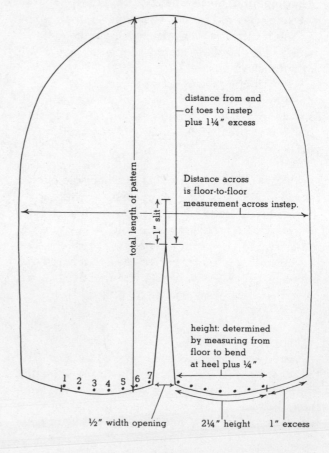

distance from end of toes to instep plus 1¼″ excess

total length of pattern

Distance across is floor-to-floor measurement across instep.

1″ slit

height: determined by measuring from floor to bend at heel plus ¼″

1 2 3 4 5 6 7

½″ width opening

2¼″ height

1″ excess

The openings, backs, and portions of the sides of the two adult patterns are reproduced here. You will have to measure your foot and fill in the toe area of the patterns. The outer edges of the pattern need only be big enough to cover your foot with enough excess to mold the shoe. The sample child's pattern is complete, but should be measured against any child to make sure it will fit.

To draw the outer or toe portions of your pattern you'll need two foot measurements: (1) from the top of your instep to the tip of your toes and (2) the width of your instep from floor to floor. Measure from the start of the opening—where the slit begins —over your instep to your toes to get the first measurement and add 1½ inches. By connecting the mark you make from this measurement with the 4-inch back pieces and the sides and by copying the shape of the child's pattern, your pattern will probably be ample. Double-check it with your instep width measurement to make sure you have plenty of leather to cover the foot with an inch left over on each side. The excess is a total waste of very good leather, but it is needed for molding. Cut the pattern in paper, cutting out the hole and slitting the slit 2 inches, and try the paper on to check again. The slit will eventually be the lace area of the shoe and will be lengthened after the molding.

Engineering these opening patterns is a great deal more challenging than it would appear from the little, ready-made holes given here. If you want to try it yourself later on, here are some of the whys of patternmaking so you can understand the theory.

How the finished shoe undulates around the anklebone and over the instep is directly related to the size of the hole.

Notice the pattern opening. It involves three measurements: (1) width of the opening, (2) length of the opening, and (3) the distance between the two sides at the back, plus the 2-inch slit which provides room for your foot during molding and becomes the lace area. The length of the opening is based on how high up on the instep the shoe is to come. The width determines where it will undercut the ankles, but is related to the third measurement, the distance separating the parts of the back. This distance directly affects the spread of the slit when it is finally stretched over the foot. The wider the distance between the two sides, the less spread at the instep. No matter how far apart the backs are on the pattern, you will sew them together to create the 3-inch height of the shoe. The wider the opening, the more leather you cut away at the back, and that leaves more leather to cover the instep. Think about it and try experimental patterns to get the concept.

We have often used a front-opening pattern, an expanded version of the child's pattern. This did not undercut the ankles; it covered them in a way similar to the fit of a desert boot. On high-arched peo-

Front Opening Pattern for Adult Shoes

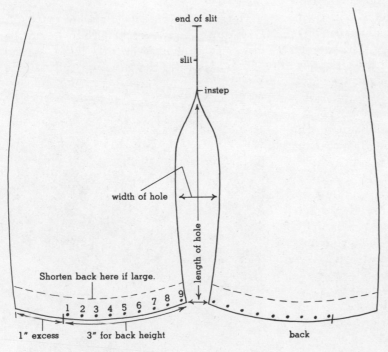

end of slit

slit

instep

width of hole

length of hole

Shorten back here if large.

1 2 3 4 5 6 7 8 9

1″ excess   3″ for back height

back

Trace pattern on solid lines, finish toe area to fit your foot, and cut out.

Length of hole = distance from heel tendon to instep.

Length of hole + distance from instep to toe end + 1½″ will determine total length of pattern. Connect length with 4″ width marks at back to draw out total pattern.

ple the two sides of the lace area ended up widely separated and sometimes looked strange and unnatural. Thus we developed the interesting tabs, rings, and other add-on pieces to narrow the actual space. I've tried patterns that go higher at the heel, truly like a desert boot, but they had too much bag and bulk at the instep and never fit. If you want something higher over the ankles, plan to add a separate top. Otherwise, the upper must be made in two pieces—more difficult to fit and work with.

Cutting Out and Sewing the Uppers

After you've drawn and cut out your paper pattern, select the leather for your shoes. Select a quality portion of the hide, without imperfections and with consistent grain and thickness. Cut the two patterns out side by side on the hide to achieve the matched grain which is the mark of a good shoe. Do remember to flip the pattern, particularly the side opening, which has a definite right and left. The tongue and reinforcement pieces will be cut later.

To sew the backs together, refer to pages 48–49 on moccasins—the steps and processes are identical. Once you have sewn them, the tops or uppers will be ready for molding.

MOLDING THE SHOES

Here is the part of shoemaking which will make you feel like "ze artiste" at work. It is very important to do a good job at this stage, so don't get so carried away with your image that you forget to notice all of the details involved. I mention this because it is the one time in the making of the shoe when you will meet the customer for a fitting before the shoes are finished or look like shoes. There you are humbly kneeling at his feet, anxious to do a good job, and a customer will start complaining about something. It is a psychologically bad position in which to handle complaints, and consequently you can easily get flustered. Most customers are awfully nice and realize this might be a moment of anxiety for you, but some of them (even your family and friends) can launch into commentary that they don't even think of as a complaint but will set you off until you forget everything. Don't let them get to you. Act as if you know exactly what you are doing and take your time to do it properly. If you aren't satisfied with the molding you get the first time, take the shoe apart and repeat the process until it is right. You can, of course, do the molding for your own shoes on your own feet, but it is awkward and there is

more chance of error. Of course you won't be complaining either.

First get everything glued and ready. The uppers and bottoms must be glued so they will stick together. Apply a ½-inch margin around the edge of the bottoms. On the uppers you must spread a large margin, far more than you will use, but you have no idea where the molding line will fall. Look at the picture (below) to see the approximate area of the upper to be covered with glue. Begin at hole 1 of the stitching at the back and work your way around with the glue. Make your margin of glue wider and wider as you move forward on the shoe, until you have glue about 3 inches in from the toe. This glue will not hurt your feet and actually acts as a waterproofer. Then wait until the glue on all four pieces is dry.

The molding process is simple but important. It boils down to the idea that you want to shape and press and stretch the leather into a shoe over the foot and glue it to the top edge of the bottom piece

with as few wrinkles, gathers, or bags as you can manage. When the heel, back area, and toe area are properly positioned and stretched, the sides will almost automatically fall into place.

If the shoes will always be worn with socks, mold the shoes over thin socks. They will not stick to the glued leather. Always seat the person being fitted in a low chair with plenty of floor space for you to crawl around on. If you're molding for yourself stand with your foot on a stool.

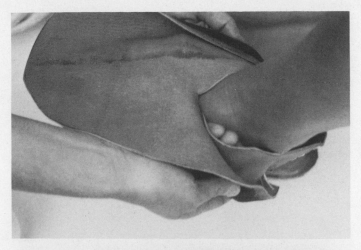

If you are making a pattern with a side opening, match the left upper with the left bottom and right with right. The slit should point toward the little toe. Curl up the bottom portion of the upper to get it flexing and closer to the shape you will finally be giving it.

Slip the upper over the foot and up the leg. If the opening is not large enough to get the foot in, lengthen the slit a little bit, no more than you have to. Position the foot on the shoe bottom, with the knee directly above the ankle and the leg straight. Don't let the customer move. You must do the bending and twisting. Move the heel slightly forward on the bottom so that you can bend around and get a clear view of the center mark on the bottom and an inch on either side of the mark.

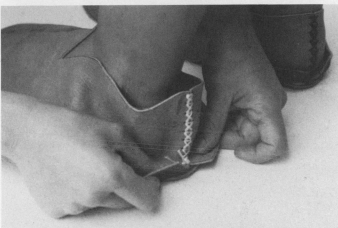

Place the upper over the bottom so that the center of the stitching on the upper rests on the center line of the bottom about ¼ inch in from the edge. Press down the upper leather for an inch on either side of the stitching, following the contours of the bottom.

Now have the person move his heel back into the proper position on the bottom, and simultaneously pull on the toe portion so that the leather is taut and snug against the heel.

Concentrate on the toe area. Lift the upper, position the foot properly on the bottom, and line up the openings. A side-opening slit should point between the little toe and the next, a front opening between the big toe and the next, or along the middle of the foot.

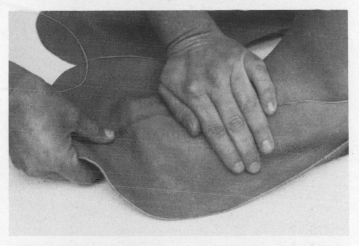

Now stretch and pull the leather forward over the toes until you can see the outline of the toes under the leather. Put your left hand (if you are right-handed) very, very firmly over the instep to hold the leather in the stretched position, and have the person gently flex his toe just a bit to stretch the leather slightly, giving him the toe room he requires. You don't have to allow very much. The leather will stretch as the shoes are worn and the padding packs down. Now quickly press the upper leather down onto the bottom, following the contour of the toe area and keeping your left hand tight over the instep.

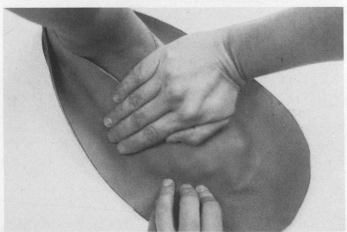

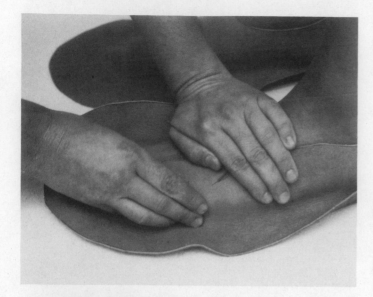

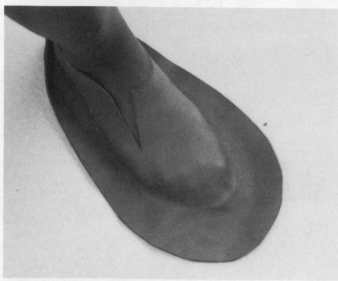

At this point, you should have a nearly molded shoe which fits snugly at the heel and toe but still allows some toe room. Keep your hand on the instep and, working from toe to heel, pull the leather down at the sides until it falls into place along the edge of the bottom. Push and knead and try to compress and work the leather so that there are no marked wrinkles. If there are wrinkles—the heavier the leather, the more you will have—space them evenly so they aren't all in one spot. Make sure you get the leather molded tight to the foot along the sides to eliminate the bags that might occur around the opening.

When the molding is finished, press all around the edges again to set the leather firmly in place. Do the second shoe and compare them. Are they similar? Do they conform tightly and completely around the heel? (Redo it if not.) Do they bag anywhere? Is there too much toe room in front? Check and examine the shoe carefully. When you are satisfied, have the customer remove the shoes gently. Try not to disrupt the molding, but if this should happen, turn the shoe upside down and you will be able to see a line where the upper was glued to the bottom. Pinch it back in place.

When the shoe is off the foot, turn it over and examine it to be certain everything is in order. Sometimes you haven't made the margin of glue on the upper wide enough and it isn't set in that spot. Just slip a little glue along the bare spot, let it dry, and press the leather into the place where it naturally falls.

If the shoe seemed to be too tight and fitted into every crevice on the foot, don't worry about it. After it is sewn, you will take a strong stick or hammer handle and unstick from the inside all the leather that isn't sewed down.

Let the glue dry throughly before you cut away the excess leather from the edges.

REMOVING EXCESS LEATHER

After the glue on the molded shoe has had at least 15 minutes to bond the surfaces thoroughly, you can cut away all the excess leather from around the edges. Your goal is to remove the leather so that the edges of the bottom and the upper are even and you will be able to follow the shape of the bottom and outline of the shoe easily when you nail or sew. You need some very sharp shears or a sharp knife for this job. Just cut away the excess, keeping the shears or blade parallel to the edge of the bottom so the two pieces are even. Start cutting at the heel, and try not to have any jagged cuts.

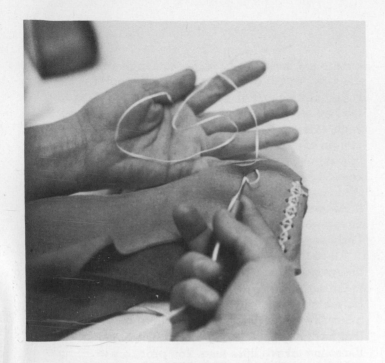

If there was a lot of excess, indicate on your pattern where you could have used less.

Once the excess is off you are ready to sew or nail.

ATTACHING THE UPPER
TO THE BOTTOM

SEWING THE SHOES. This looks hard but isn't. You need the stitching awl (see page 20), good, heavy thread, and an hour or so for some peaceful, hassle-free, noise-free stitching in the sun or by the fire, or wherever you're comfortable.

Sew from the top of the shoe (or sandal) to the bottom, beginning around the heel area. Start in the usual way with a ½-inch tail of thread to allow for the mass of three or four thicknesses and pick up the tail to make your "bobbin." Pull out enough thread to go approximately twice around the shoe for your bobbin thread. If this seems an unwieldy length, use what is comfortable. If you run out of thread you can tie it off on the bottom and begin again with no one the wiser. Sew evenly ¼ inch in from the edge.

Try to make the stitching nice. People will see it, and you want to be proud of it. Smaller stitches make it easier to sew around the toe area and rounded portions.

It is best to sit so that you can really bear down on the awl handle, twisting the needle and keeping your fingers right under the spot where it will penetrate to add pressure until you feel the point coming through. Then instantly move your fingers aside.

There's only one important mistake you can make here, other than not keeping an even ¼ inch from the edge. Watch the angle of your needle as you insert it. While you are following a straight stitch line on top, the needle can enter at an angle and make an uneven stitch line underneath. Its being uneven isn't the problem—the concern is that the stitching on the bottom might be closer to the edge than it is on the top. After you have applied the sole you will sand the edges and you can't afford to sand through any stitching.

NAILING THE SHOES. In order to nail shoes, with or without a midsole, you'll need two thin strips of latigo—not soft leather and not a thong—about ¼ inch or ³⁄₁₆ inch wide and long enough to go around the shoe. The purpose of this strip, or welt, is to give added strength. It helps to distribute the pressure of the nails evenly along the edge and to keep the upper leather from being pried loose by the enormous strain the foot exerts.

Start nailing the welt on at the inner edge of the instep, where the beginning and end will not show much. Nail in both directions. Don't try to glue the strip on—it is too small—just nail it into place along the edge of the shoe, spacing the nails ½ to ⅝ inch apart. Practice nailing a strip to a spare piece of leather before you begin on your shoe. It requires some finger pressure to keep the welt where you want it, place the nail, and get the whole thing tight and even.

FINISHING

After sewing or nailing the shoes you can finish the work on either the uppers or the bottoms. I prefer leather until they are as high as you want and sand the taper evenly. However, you cannot go just as high as you want. The highest I've tried was 2 inches, low by wedgie standards, and this attempt was a total failure. Weight is your enemy. Even using crepe, the lightest-weight soling, when you layer it up that much your result is an extremely heavy shoe. Assuming that the purpose of making the wedge high is to create an elevated but delicate shoe, you have done the opposite of your goal by making a clunker. All commercial high heels and wedgies and clogs are hollow inside and made from the lightest-weight plastics and wood and molded rubber. If you have a complete woodworking shop, you might be able to create high wedges from balsa wood, or something equally lightweight.

The "high" wedge shown on page 69 is only about an inch high, including the sole. Three layers of 15-iron crepe. It is very comfortable and sporty-looking, but that or perhaps another ¼ inch is just as high as you can go.

High heels. Making shoes or boots with heels higher than ½ inch requires some mastery of the inner secrets of shoemaking, some additional equipment, and an understanding of what you are doing. In other words, high heels are advanced, and you'll be disappointed if you attempt them before you have accomplished the easier work.

An S-shaped steel shank must be inserted in any shoe with a high heel. This rigid piece of metal creates and retains the slope of the arch from the top of the heel to the floor level of the shoe. Without this shank, the arch would fall to floor level like a stair step rather than retain the traditional gentle descent. Shanks are made and sold in many shapes and sizes; which one you select depends on the height of the heel you have chosen.

The simplest use of a shank would be in a work boot or shoe with a ⅝-inch heel. The shank gives the shoe added strength and support and prevents any movement or play at the heel. You can nail this low shank to the inside of any kind of soling, including crepe. Simply fit the shank so that it goes from behind the ball of the foot to some point well over the center of the heel. Use a clinching nail at either end to secure it and attach the upper over the sole as you normally would.

The process becomes more difficult with a higher 2- or 3-inch heel. You must use leather soling for its strength and pliability. You must also use a heel that is not hollow so that you can nail both it and the shank to the sole.

Heels and shanks are sold at shoe findings stores and should be selected together. Create the heel shape of your sole pattern by tracing around the top of the heel so that the two will fit together as one unit. Cut out the sole and glue the heel to its outside. When the heel has been glued, nail it to the sole from the inside, using fairly long nails so that the heel will not pull off when it is worn. Be careful to keep the nails straight. If driven in at an angle, nails can come out one side of the heel or, if the heel is wood, can split the heel.

Now comes the tricky part: attaching the shank. The higher the heel is and the smaller the foot, the more difficult this will be to do properly. If it is not done properly, the shoe will always "walk," which means that when you have weight on your toes, the heel isn't firmly on the ground so the pressure of your foot pushes the shoe forward. It is annoying and the shoe never feels right.

Soak the sole-heel combination in water until the sole is pliable. Attach the shank to the inside of the sole at about the middle of the heel, push the arch of the sole until it cleaves to the contours of the shank, then nail the sole into position somewhere behind the ball of the foot. Look to see that both the heel and the ball part of the shoe lie flat on the ground. Test it by putting your foot on it to see if it walks. If it does, take off the shank and keep fitting it until there is no play between the heel and sole. They should be rigid. Let the sole dry thoroughly and then attach the upper to it with glue or nails.

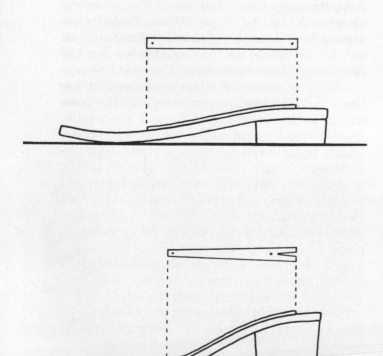

Finishing the Edges

SANDING. The purpose of sanding the edges is to smooth them out so they look nice. Sanding is done after you have attached the sole to the midsole so that you can sand all the miscellaneous layers of leather and soling and transform them into one continuous edge. You also have the opportunity during this step to reshape the shoe slightly so that offending angles, such as points at the toes or wide sides, can be trimmed to be more pleasing to you.

If you don't have a power sander (see page 22), it is a laborious but not impossible job to get the edges smooth. Use anything—including rough concrete—to get the worst of the edges smooth and then heavy- and fine-grit sandpaper to finish them. Some former students who live in a van and sell shoes at craft fairs manage everything without the power sander, so it can be done; it is just a chore.

With the power sander it is a snap. Hold the shoe firmly perpendicular to the drum so you do not sand on an angle. Keep the leather of the uppers out of the way so you don't nick them in the process. Be very careful not to sand through the stitches on a sewn shoe, or everything will start to unravel. The wheel goes rapidly, and the sanding can go faster and deeper than you want if you don't pay attention. The leather parts—midsole, lining, upper—sand more slowly than crepe, so you have to equalize the pressure to get them even.

BURNISHING. This is the final process in your work on the sole. It is done merely for the aesthetic value of giving the edge of the sole, mainly leather, a polished, finished look. You simply apply dye to the edges, then polish and brush.

If you have used a white soling, you'll probably want to leave everything the natural color and just apply a natural, colorless polish or beeswax to the edge so it looks shiny.

If you've used a dark soling, black or brown, dye the leather part of the edge with a matching color. I prefer black because it truly penetrates the pores of the leather and dyes it completely; brown dyes look rather opaque. After you've applied the dye, cover the entire edge with a polish the same color or beeswax. Rub it in to fill up any cracks. Then brush, brush, brush, until it glistens and shines. Bark-tanned soling really burnishes well, and you feel like a master craftsperson, but even crepe is improved by this process. The shoe should now look super, and you should be proud to wear it.

If you still have work to do on the upper parts of the shoe—reinforcement pieces and so on—it is a good idea to wait to burnish these edges until you finish, since you can get dirty while holding and working on dyed shoes. Wash your hands after using all this dye, or the dye will end up places you don't want it to be.

Finishing the Uppers

Put the shoe on and try it. It is probably too tight and you had trouble getting into it. The slit or lace area is not long enough, does not expand to allow easy entry. Mark a point on the leather at the *widest part of your foot,* the ball. Mark the point on both shoes before cutting. Then cut, continuing the slit to your mark. When you are satisfied that the slit has been

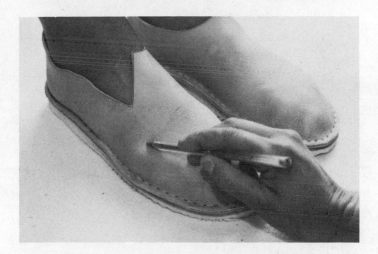

opened far enough, no farther than the ball, punch a very small hole at the base of the cut to distribute any pressure that may be exerted at this point to prevent the leather from ripping or tearing.

If the shoe is to become a boot, make the pattern for your top or boot portion. If it is to stay a low shoe, read on.

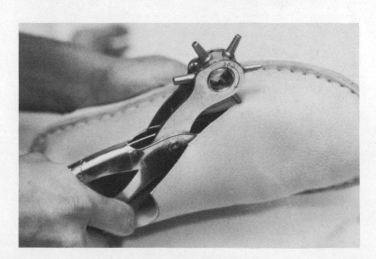

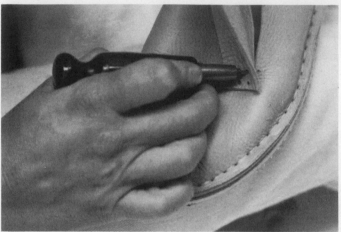

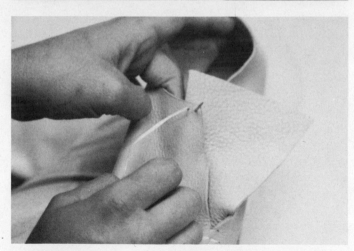

TONGUE. The tongue consists of three measurements: width at the base of the opening (the part nearest your toes), width at the top (nearest your leg), and the distance between the two. At the top it is much wider than the base, and thus the tongue looks like a triangle with a point cut off: a trapezoid. The tongue will underlap the other shoe material, like any other tongue. At the top, measure the width you will need and add 1 inch extra (½ inch per side) for the underlap. Measure the length and add 1 inch to allow for attaching and some extra just in case. At the base, the amount of material allotted should be minimal—1 inch on the side-opener and 1½ inches on the front; excess here cannot be easily lopped off and will dig into your foot. Once you've made a paper pattern, try it on, cut it out of leather, and sew it on.

The sewing part can be a real chore unless you've prepunched holes for the stitcher to penetrate and you don't have to feel your way around inside the shoe to punch them. It's a simple matter of punching them along the base of the tongue (about ⅛ inch in from the edge)—generally four or five holes will do it—and then putting these holes over the appropriate spot on the shoe, transferring them with a pen or an awl, and punching them with the awl. You then have two sets of holes ready to be sewn together. To determine the appropriate spot on your shoe, punch a hole in the tongue, centered and ½ inch up from the base edge. Then match up this centered hole with the one you made at the base of the slit, center the tongue, and the holes are appropriately placed. Sew the tongue inside the shoe, using either a stitcher or needle and thread, and *make sure the knot is on the outside* of the shoe.

On the side-opening model, place a small holding stitch on the topside of the lace opening to position the ½-inch underlap permanently. Otherwise the tongue will fall to the side.

Wait until your laces are in before you cut off the excess leather on the tongue.

COUNTERS OR FOXINGS. Shoes should have some reinforcement at the heel to provide extra strength to the heel, which gets a lot of abuse, and to give added support to discourage sideways motion. An inside reinforcement piece is called a counter and an outside one a foxing. I prefer to use the foxing, because it covers the stitching, and you can do many creative things with this piece, adding interest.

You could put foxings on before molding, but there are drawbacks. Frequently in molding you end up with a crooked stitch line at the back. This doesn't affect fit, but it looks bad and the foxing covers it up. If the shoe stretches or is too large at the heel, it is a simple matter to remove the foxing, cut the stitching, make your alteration, and put the foxing back on. If the foxing is permanently sewn on first, thus sewn to the bottom together with the upper, it is far more difficult to remove when you try to make your repair.

I think a foxing or counter is best if it circles the whole heel, although we've made them much smaller, particularly on double-layered shoes that are already fairly heavy. Make it as high as the back, or make it higher and create a pull tab. You are free to create anything you want back here, as long as you add something to provide reinforcement. Just make a paper pattern, play around with the shape you want, examine the illustrations of our shoes for ideas, cut the pattern out in leather, glue it on, and sew it. You cannot sew it around the bottom edge; just glue it there so that it covers the bottom of the stitching.

A counter can be nothing more than a piece of leather you glue inside the heel area. It is easy to do, but doesn't add any fun or interest. I believe in putting my work where it will show.

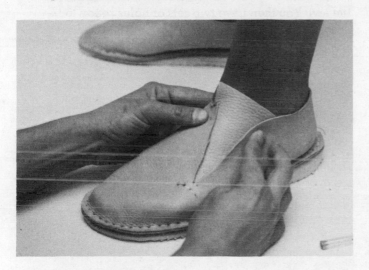

REINFORCEMENT PIECES. Here is another area where you can be creative, and your work will serve the purpose of reinforcing the lace area and the top edges of the opening if you feel it is needed. A reinforcement piece is a nice but not necessary addition to the shoe. Eyelets can be used to strengthen the lace holes so they won't pull out of shape. Your reinforcement pieces can change an otherwise dull shoe into a unique creation. The almost too unique piece on the "high" wedge shoe was added to cover a blotch of dye spilled on the

toe and proves that no error is so bad it cannot be dealt with somehow.

Design reinforcement pieces by using the original pattern, marking off the area you have to work with (by measuring the molded shoe), and drawing out your design from there. Check it out on the shoe to make sure it is big enough (the opening may have stretched larger during the molding), cut it out of the leather, glue it on, and sew. At times it takes patience to sew it on in the hard-to-get area down by the toe and beyond the lace opening, but it isn't impossible. I never add these before molding because I never know how my original vision is going to look until the shoe is more like a shoe and I can see if it's come out the way I imagined it.

ALTERING THE SHOE. If, during all this adding of pieces and fitting, you feel there are changes to be made, make them. If the shoe feels too high in the back, remove the stitches and cut it down. If the shoe feels too high around the ankle, or one side looks (is) higher than the other, carefully trim away the offending portion. To match up the two shoes, use the leather trimmed from one as a pattern in trimming the other.

PLACING THE LACE HOLES. When you are satisfied that you've added all the trim and reinforcement you want, the final step is to punch the lace holes. Put the shoe on and draw the sides of leather together until they fit your foot, don't bag on the sides, and feel tight and snug. Generally, the higher up your instep the lacing goes, the better it will fit. Make marks on both shoes indicating the top lace holes. Position your holes nearest the base of the tongue as close to it as possible, and fill in the area with equidistant marks, about an inch or less apart. The number depends on the size of lacing you've selected. If you want thin little laces, use more holes and small holes appropriate for the size of the laces. Thick leather thongs get bigger and fewer holes.

The holes for side-opening shoes should not be

opposite each other on both sides. That is, the top hole is best positioned at the top of the curve, above the other top sole. Trim off the tongue so that it is underneath all the laces.

BREAKING THE SHOES IN

Usually new shoes are very tight at first. I have never made a pair for myself that I did not think was too tight when I first put them on. A breaking-in period is generally essential. Don't let your blood pressure rise just because they feel tight: they should be, and they will stretch. Prepare your customers for this tightness, or you'll be in for a very tense period while they mentally debate with themselves about paying you. Make them walk around and start breaking them in, and in a week or two they will be bringing in their friends for a pair.

There are some things you can do to hasten the breaking-in process. Take a hammer handle or something narrow and strong and jam it around the toe to stretch it out. The thicker the leather the more jamming you'll have to do.

If the shoes will not darken and be ruined—test a scrap—oil them. Lexol mixed with a little alcohol is ideal for this. Spray it on and work it in. The heat from the foot will hasten the stretching of the leather.

Powder inside the shoes so the foot slips in without resistance.

Wear thin socks at first and work up to thicker ones.

Often a very real problem is irritation from the stitches in the tongue and the heel, and back stitches just uneven enough to pull down the sock at the heel. Find a small piece of metal to slip inside the shoe, under the stitches, and hammer them hard. Hammering not only levels the stitches, it mashes down the leather so it lies comfortably on the foot without digging in.

WHAT WENT WRONG?

If your shoes are too big, your sole pattern was probably too big, your foot drawing was inaccurate, or the molding was not tight enough. You can remove the foxing, cut open the stitching, tighten up the backs, and restitch. You can also do this if the shoes stretch out with wear and get too big.

If the shoes are too small and you have worn them conscientiously, you can change the soling on them, or sand down the thickness if it is crepe. Thinner soling will make them more flexible—they will move and bend more readily.

You can remove the foxing and add a wedge of leather at the heel to provide more room. Both of these procedures are rarely necessary. Generally the shoes just need to be worn.

If you do need to change the soling, get some glue thinner and wipe it around the edges of the shoe where it joins the midsole. The thinner will gradually dissolve the glue, and after repeated applications you will be able to pry it off with a screwdriver or something similar. It takes time and is messy, but will be worth the effort.

If your shoes or sandals are not as perfect on the first attempt as you had hoped, please don't throw them away or burn them. Put them aside for a few days until you have cooled down, then get them out and rework them till you are satisfied.

SHOE VARIATIONS

Children's Shoes

Exactly like adult shoes, but in miniature. Don't try to make them fancy or cute, just concentrate on fit. With small children—under 70 pounds—I generally eliminate padding. The thick padding used for adults is too thick for lighter-weight children to pack down and the shoe will be too tight. Very little

kids of three and four do not even have the foot muscles to twist their feet into a slightly tight shoe, so keep it loose. Moccasins are probably the better choice for these young'uns.

When you eliminate the padding, you can eliminate the lining and the midsole serves as both. It is possible to sew two layers of leather on a good home sewing machine and therefore possible to pop out a pair of shoes in a couple of hours.

SOLE PATTERN.   Do the usual foot drawing for the child and make the sole pattern from this, following the shape of the foot. Add about ⅝ inch toe room, or ½ inch if the feet are very small. Stay exactly on the lines of the drawing at the ball area, go in slightly to create an arch, and shape the heel so it is rounded, but stay on the lines of the drawing. When you draw around the foot with a pen, the width you pick up is proportionately much greater with a small child's foot than with an adult's. Thus you don't have to add extra room around the ball or the heel.

Use a lightweight soling that is flexible; 9 to 12 iron is about as thick as children can use.

UPPER PATTERN.   A sample child's pattern is included (see page 62) to give you a starting point from which to expand or decrease. Measure the feet from instep to toes, and add 1 inch. Measure the thickness of the instep and add excess, about 2 inches. Measure the height to the tendon, generally about 2¼ to 2¾ inches.

Do everything else—molding, sewing, and so on—as you would for an adult.

Golf Shoes

It has never seemed to make any sense that in a game such as golf, which involves miles and miles of walking and demands foot flexibility, particularly in the tippy-toe swinging position, the shoe should be the stiffest, hardest shoe made. The golf shoe shown above is a standard, regular, soft-leather side-opener reinforced at the heel and the lace holes, but has a sole with golf spikes inserted.

The sole can be made in one of two ways. Shoe findings stores do sell golf soles ready to attach to a shoe. However, these come in definite sizes with the bases of the upper already attached in a pattern around the edge of the sole. Thus the size and shape is predetermined. The "from scratch" method is probably easier and cheaper and you'll have your pattern as you design it.

The spikes come in two parts. The bases are

T-nuts, which are sold separately from the spikes. These T-nuts are inserted and screwed into drilled holes in the bottom of the sole, which should be of leather or Neolite, strong enough to take the strain of the spikes. After you have inserted these bases in a pattern in the sole, make the shoe up as usual, either nailing it or sewing it and gluing the sole onto the midsole. When the shoe is finished, you simply screw in the spikes, which come in men's or ladies' sizes. Very simple.

I can't absolutely guarantee that this soft, flexible design will lower your score, but the customers who have dared depart from the conventional designs swear it makes their game far more enjoyable and comfortable. They can forgo the electric cart and walk the course comfortably and enjoyably.

Bowling Shoes

The popular ones sold in bowling alleys use a chrome leather sole which is flexible enough for all the movement of bowling, but slick enough to skid. Just make an upper design of your choice and glue (don't nail) the chrome sole to the bottom.

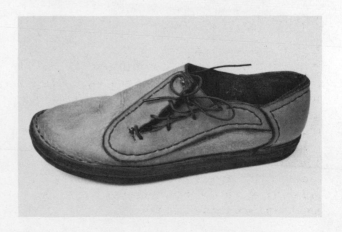

Jogging Shoes

This is a frank copy of commercial versions. The pattern involves some measuring. It starts with a front opening with an allowance to undercut the ankles (like the side opening). The slit in front ex-tends about 1 inch past the ball of the foot toward the toe area. The front of the toe area has a rein-forcement piece that keeps the foot from pushing beyond the end of the shoe.

The entire shoe—tongue, lace holes, foxing, stitching, and reinforcement pieces—is assembled prior to molding. Mold with the laces in place so the opening doesn't stretch.

The stitching was done on a machine and is prin-cipally decorative, although there is the hope that it might prevent stretch on the sides. It is generally possible to stitch through at least one layer, if not two, of leather on a home sewing machine equipped with a leather roller foot and a leather machine needle (three-sided point). If you do not have a machine, the stitching can be done by hand or eliminated and the reinforcement pieces glued into place.

The tongue is lined inside with a thin piece of sheepskin to protect the top of the foot from the pressure of the laces.

The shoe is handsewn with one layer of gristle 9-iron rubber soling glued to the midsole.

Boots

Bootmaking is the height of shoemaking sophistication. Appropriately, it is the most difficult and demanding part of shoemaking. It is relatively easy if you want to make a boot from a moccasin or shoe. You simply design a low top or a high top (as high as 12 inches from the floor) and add it to the base. These boot tops—and the patterns described here—are one piece, lace up the front, and are no particular challenge once you have mastered the principles of their design.

A boot that envelops the calf muscle, such as a stovepipe or a form-fitting contoured boot, is created from a pattern of two or more pieces and a base specifically designed to be the base for the boot and is infinitely more difficult than the first type. Don't try it till you feel advanced or you will be terribly disappointed and discouraged. If you do attempt this type, you will probably be trying to copy some of the fashionable commercial boot styles that appeal to you and therefore I have not included any patterns for these types, only suggestions for adapting the commercial styles to your handmade methods. To create patterns for these, get a photograph of the boot you want and copy it.

MAKING BOOTS FROM MOCCASINS

Your goal is to develop a pattern that will match the bottom portion of the moccasin and fit the leg. The moccasin is slightly easier to do, so we'll take that first. The top will be attached at the ends of the ball line, on an angle, overlapping the heel by ½ inch. Try to develop the pattern so that the top does not fit skintight at the ankle and inhibit movement. The portions above the ankle and at the instep should be designed to fit so that there is approximately a 1-inch front opening all the way up the top to provide for the laces and tongue and leave room for stretch. Thus you will add material at the ankle and instep and subtract material, based on the measurements of the leg, above the ankle. To do this patternwork you'll use a large piece of paper folded in half (or two pieces 8½ by 11 taped together) so you can make half the pattern, cut it out, open it up, and have the whole. After setting up the paper drawing on the critical measurement points of the moccasin,

ankle, and leg, you will measure the moccasin and the leg and transfer these measurements to the paper.

Setting Up the Paper

Use a large piece of paper, folded. The fold represents the back of the pattern; the bottom edge represents the floor.

Measuring from the floor line up, make marks at the following intervals: 1½ inches up, 2½ inches, 4 inches, 6 inches, 8 inches, and 10 inches. At the 1½-inch mark, draw a line completely across the page, parallel to the floor line.

Measuring Your Moccasin and Leg

First, with a tape, measure your completed moccasin from one end of the ball line to the other around the heel (see page 38). Note this measurement on

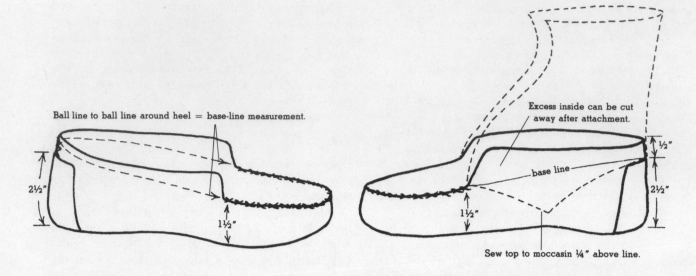

Ball line to ball line around heel = base-line measurement.

2½"

1½"

Excess inside can be cut away after attachment.

base line

½"

2½"

1½"

Sew top to moccasin ¼" above line.

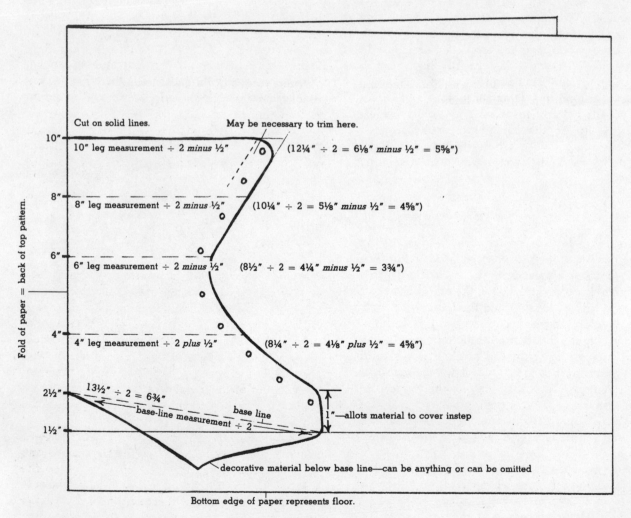

Cut on solid lines.

May be necessary to trim here.

10"

10" leg measurement ÷ 2 *minus* ½"   (12¼" ÷ 2 = 6⅛" *minus* ½" = 5⅝")

8"

8" leg measurement ÷ 2 *minus* ½"   (10¼" ÷ 2 = 5⅛" *minus* ½" = 4⅝")

6"

6" leg measurement ÷ 2 *minus* ½"   (8½" ÷ 2 = 4¼" *minus* ½" = 3¾")

Fold of paper = back of top pattern.

4"

4" leg measurement ÷ 2 *plus* ½"   (8¼" ÷ 2 = 4⅛" *plus* ½" = 4⅝")

2½"

13½" ÷ 2 = 6¾"

base line

base-line measurement ÷ 2

1"—allots material to cover instep

1½"

decorative material below base line—can be anything or can be omitted

Bottom edge of paper represents floor.

Scale   ½" = 1"

the paper at the 2½-inch mark. This is your baseline measurement.

Standing in bare feet, using a straight ruler, mark your leg with a pen at 4 inches from the floor (or about 1 inch above the ankle), then 6 inches, 8 inches, etc. Measure to as high or as low as you want the boot top to reach, and at 2-inch intervals between. Now measure around the leg at those marks, using a tape or a string, and transfer the measurements to the appropriate spot on the paper. Divide *all* measurements in half, because you are creating half the pattern. The resulting numbers I will call half measurements.

Developing the Pattern

This is hard to visualize, so study the illustration carefully.

The 2½-inch mark on the paper represents the heel of your moccasin (which was designed to be 3 inches high, and you now want a ½-inch overlap); the 1½-inch line represents the height at the ball or the thickness of the moccasin. To establish your base line, which represents the angle on your moccasin at which the heel falls to the ball line, you must connect the 2½-inch mark with a line that hits somewhere along the 1½-inch line.

Use your half-base-line measurement and a ruler and start at the 2½-inch mark. Find the point along the 1½-inch line where the measurement intersects and draw a line connecting the points. The 1-inch drop on paper equals the angle on the moccasin. This angled line I'll call your base line.

At the end of the base line, where it meets the 1½-inch line, draw a 1-inch line up, 90 degrees from the 1½-inch line, to allow material to go up and over the instep; angle the line slightly (⅛ inch) toward the fold of the paper.

At the 4-inch mark, or ankle, *add* ½ inch to your half measurement and draw a line out from the fold of the paper equal to that number (half measurement plus ½ inch).

At the 6-inch mark, and any others which may be above it, *subtract* ½ inch from your half measurement and draw lines out those lengths.

Connect the ends of all the lines with a gentle, nonangular curving line.

Below the base line you can add decorative points or curves or whatever you think might be more interesting than a straight line for the base—or you can leave it as is. Be careful not to add any extra at the heel or much at the sides of the ball, the important attachment points.

Cut the folded pattern out, both sides at one time, so they will be the same. Fit the paper pattern on the moccasin and the leg to see how it fits. If you can't get an idea, cut out a sample in fabric, which fits a lot better than paper. Should the distance between the two edges where the leather will come together be greater than 1 inch, but even all the way up, your pattern is probably okay, since the leather will stretch and be pulled together by the laces. The important factor is that the boot top fits around the moccasin, meeting exactly at the ends of the ball line and overlapping the heel ½ inch. If the rest is too big, you can always cut it down, but it is so hard to add on. If you feel you need more material over the instep, make a new pattern extending the 1-inch line up from the base-line end and making it longer than 1 inch.

Cutting Out the Leather

When you are satisfied that the pattern is accurate, or even a little big, cut out one in leather and fit that to the moccasin and leg. Trim where you need to and change your pattern accordingly so you will know what you have done for future boots and for the second top piece.

When you've got a good leather piece ready to attach, you can design and add trim or reinforcement pieces along the edges where the laces will be and around the top. If you want fringe or a fold-over design at the top of the boot, design this and incorporate it into your pattern. Glue and sew such pieces onto the boot top before sewing the top to the moccasin; it's a lot easier. Don't punch lace holes until the boot is assembled.

Attaching the Top

Holding the top in position at the corners and heel (it's easier with two people) and making sure both sides are even and not tilted, draw or score around the edges to indicate the glue line. Apply glue to the top and around the line you drew on the moccasin, glue the pieces together, and sew them on with your stitcher. After they have been sewn together, you can cut away any excess moccasin leather on the inside, if or when you want to. Or glue it to the top for reinforcement.

If you didn't initially plan a top, you'll have to add on to the tongue. Just cut an extension long enough to cover the distance up your leg to the height you want and add 2 inches to be on the safe side. The tongue should be 4 or 5 inches wide at the top. Connect the two pieces, using a cross-stitch such as you used at the heel of the moccasin.

Placing Lace Holes

I usually place them about 1 inch apart. Be sure to measure both sides so they are even and you don't end up with more on one side than on the other. It is all very easy, and makes a totally different item.

MAKING BOOTS FROM SHEEPSKIN MOCCASINS

The reason I keep suggesting you keep your pattern on the large side and cut it down is to allow for the thickness of leather. Measure your ankle. If it measures 8 inches, it will take about 8¼ inches of leather to encircle it. With leather this is a minor difference. However, if you are using sheepskin, it will take 10 inches of material to cover that same 8-inch ankle. When you design your pattern you have to take this added bulk into consideration. Unless you are a graduate engineer, you can't calculate this exactly. However, your sheepskin top pattern will come out very adequately if you *add* 1 inch to all your overall measurements. (Add ½ inch on your folded paper pattern.) If your first top comes out too big, great. You can cut it down and cut the second one exactly. However, since a sheepskin is only big enough for one pair of high moccasins, you cannot discard a top if it is too small and cut another. If it comes together with a 1-inch separation (2 inches should be maximum) it will be all right—it will pack down eventually. A sheepskin ½ inch thick will add less bulk than one ¾ inch thick. These directions are for the ¾-inch thickness and can be lessened a bit for the other.

You should have reinforcement at the lace holes because the sheepskin is so fragile and can tear.

Gluing the fuzzy sheepskin is something similar to being tarred and feathered. It can be done, however. To make gluing around the edges easier and eliminate some unnecessary bulk, shear (cut) wool from the skin along any part of the edge which will overlap the moccasin. Thus you can set or glue the top to the moccasin with the wool of the top beginning where the wool of the moccasin stops. Just cut away as much as you can, glue, attach, and sew. It is easy—just takes courage to cut into that beautiful skin.

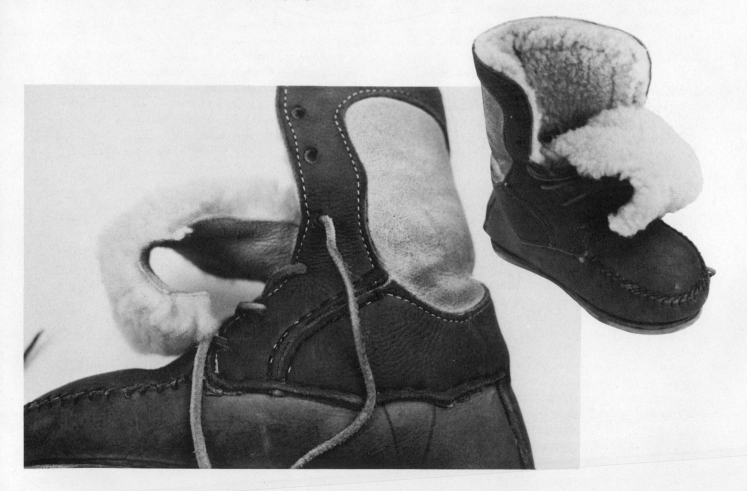

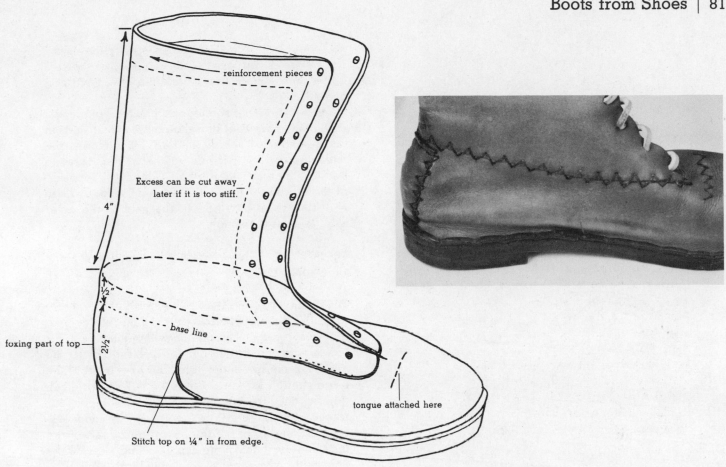

reinforcement pieces

Excess can be cut away
later if it is too stiff.

4"

½"

foxing part of top

2½"

base line

tongue attached here

Stitch top on ¼" in from edge.

MAKING BOOTS FROM SHOES

Making a boot top for a shoe is exactly the same as making a boot top for a moccasin from the ankle up. The base line is different because there is an opening down the middle of the shoe and not at the ends of the ball line. To determine your base line, start at the shoe opening and measure around the heel, adding a ½-inch overlap. The opening should have been cut on the widest part of the foot, the ball.

When you draw the pattern, the two points—heel and ball—will be nearly level and you can design your pattern measurements without the bothersome angle you needed for moccasins. To establish your base line, just draw a line straight across the paper 2½ inches up from the floor line (bottom edge of paper) and determine your pattern from there.

The foxing of the shoe can be incorporated into the pattern as in this illustration, or added separately. Draw the pattern, cut it out, fit the paper to the shoe and leg, modify if necessary, cut one side out of leather, modify it, add lace reinforcement pieces, and attach. The top should be securely attached at the end of the opening. Study the drawing and photographs.

When the top has been attached, measure the length of the tongue you will need, then add 2 inches to be safe. The width should be about 5 inches at the top. Sew the tongue in after the top is on, starting it about ½ inch before the opening.

Repeat with the other shoe.

THE STOVEPIPE BOOT

Any of the commercial varieties can be copied easily—all of them will be vastly improved upon when you make them because of the padding and the perfect fit to your calf and foot.

In developing this boot, think of it as four sections: the sole (sole, heel, and shank), the bottom (midsole, padding, and inner lining), the upper or shoe part, and the top which can go as high as your knee.

THE SOLE.   The sole will consist of a leather sole, a second "inner sole" (entirely optional), a heel, and a steel shank (see page 70). Draw your sole pattern, allowing ¾ inch beyond the longest toe,

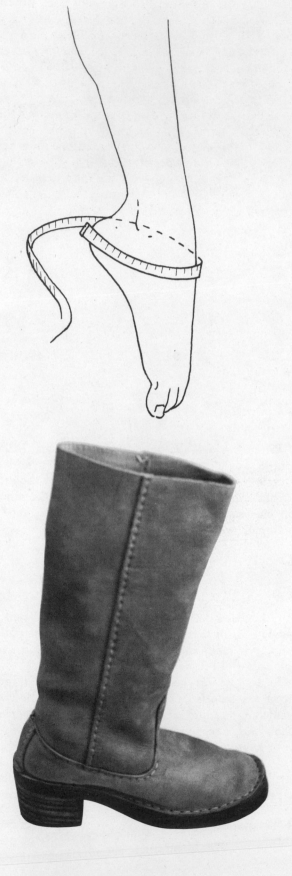

and then create the traditional square-toe shape from there if you wish. Make the heel of the sole pattern the same shape as the heel you have purchased.

The second inner sole is exactly like a wedge you might put at the heel of a shoe but this one starts at the toe and ends behind the ball. Try to feather the thickness of this half-sole so that it decreases to about ⅛ inch behind the ball. Glue it to the inside of the outer sole and sand away any excess. Then nail both soles together, fit the heel to the outer sole, and set the shank.

THE BOTTOM.   This is exactly the same as for any shoe you make.

THE UPPER OR SHOE PART.   The most important factor in this pattern, which is simply a large hole (like the front-opening type, but without any slit for laces) with the traditional tab protruding up the middle, is the size of the hole. This opening must be large enough for your foot to be withdrawn when pointed since the boot is a slip-on and you put your foot in pointed. Therefore, point your toe and measure your foot from the thickest, highest part of the instep to the back bottom part of the heel. Make your pattern opening at least this large around.

These boots should be lined. Not only will they feel silky against your leg, the lining will add the rigidity necessary to make the boot stand up without aid. It will take a lot of extra leather, time, money, and, not incidentally, glue, but it should be done. When you feel your pattern is right, cut out the leather and lining, and glue them together. Before sewing the back, test to make sure the opening is big enough, then sew the back, making the height about ¼ inch less than a shoe—about 2¾ inches.

Mold this as you would a shoe. If you are using a high heel, be sure to do the molding with the bottom placed on the sole-heel portion so that your heel is properly elevated. This changes the shape and height of the instep and puts it in the position it will be in when the boot is complete. If you plan to wear heavy socks with these, mold them over the socks.

Sew up the shoe as usual and try it on to make sure it is not uncomfortably tight at the instep. If it binds, cut it down a bit until it feels better. Glue the upper to the sole, being sure to use two applications of glue. This is the only thing holding one to the other so it should be as strong as possible.

THE TOP.   The top is one enormous cylinder which will become a cone as you fit it. Measure your calf *while standing* (the measurement while sitting is much smaller), add 1 inch, and divide the total in half. Decide what height you want the top to be. The back piece should be ½ inch longer than the desired height and the front piece 1½ inches longer. This additional inch in front is helpful in fitting the boot top to the shoe part.

Cut out all the top sections, glue them together, and stitch the fronts to the backs with one side seam. Wrap the top around your calf and leg to determine the final dimensions of the upper part of the top and staple or clip the two sides in position.

The lower portion of the top should be fitted inside the opening of the shoe, with the side seam centered, and adjusted till it fills the opening completely. Make certain the top stands straight and does not lean, and when you are satisfied, draw around the point of the opening, marking where the top fits inside the shoe. The front and back pieces will overlap a lot. Use a ruler to determine a straight seam and cut away any excess. You may cut from either piece. Cut excess leather from where the top will join the shoe, leaving a seam allowance of about ⅜ inch. The seam allowance should be as small as possible so that it won't rub your foot. Glue everything together and make sure it is correctly positioned before you sew things together. Stitching with your awl will be a laborious task because you will not be able to see the bobbin side of the stitching. Cut one of the blunt-ended needles in half and use it as a shuttle inside the boot to enable you to find the loop with your fingers.

Sandals

Sandals are fun, easy, and fast. You'll find no "what went wrong" section in this chapter—nothing can go wrong if you follow directions. Sandals require more tools than shoes or moccasins and more leather, latigo—preferably in two different thicknesses—and are not a good investment if you plan to make only one pair for yourself. They can be fairly lucrative items if you want to make some money; two or three pairs will recoup your investment and there's always someone who needs them.

After the challenge of creating shoes and moccasins in which you encase the foot completely, making a sandal is mere child's play. A pleasant 2½-hour break in the day. After creating several hundred pairs as I have done, you can become very ho-hum about being able to please people 99 percent of the time and being able to achieve perfect fits.

One reason I have become very ho-hum about sandals is that I always use one type of sandal design. I've examined hundreds of styles and designs and their fit over the years, and I still believe that this type of design is the absolute best that I can deliver. It is very rewarding to sell sandals that you know without a shadow of a doubt will always fit, even after years of wear, be durable and comfortable, and look good. People who come to you for sandals—or any footwear—often have gotten crippled just crawling from store to store looking for something that fits and is not so shoddy it will fall apart after a couple of months. They come to you for help, not a dizzying array of choice in style, and they appreciate being told what can be made well and what will be comfortable and last. By the time they've chosen one design, a color, a soling, and a buckle, they've had all the choice they want. Keep things simple. Don't make weird designs that snake all over the foot and leg—very few of them work. And don't remake designs that obviously don't fit a person just because they've become accustomed to them. They'll soon be accustomed to yours and like them much better.

Here are my dogmatic beliefs about what a sandal should be and the design to go with them.

I have used, consistently, year in and year out, continuous-strap designs. These are probably the easiest designs to make and probably the cheapest as well, but that is not the reason I have stuck with them. I can get a top perfect fit immediately, and that fit will stay that way forever. Leather stretches, particularly latigo. No matter how heavy, either in weight or width of strap, the leather will stretch and continue to do so as long as you wear it. No amount of prestretching will eliminate it. Thus, you must have a design that will be adjustable for the life of the sandal. A continuous-strap design is what it says: one continuous strap that spirals over the foot and under the top sole with the beginning and end of the strap meeting at the buckle or button. Two heel or back straps hold the ankle strap down under the bones and keep your side-to-side heel movement to a minimum; with a flexible sole on the bottom, you've made a beautiful item.

These continuous-strap designs are more durable than the heavier designs on which the straps are nailed into position. With a continuous strap the pressure is evenly distributed, and there are no nails or threads to come out after constant wearing. No part is weaker than any other part. Most custom sandalmakers have an unbudgeable idea that a sandal must be heavy to be durable—stiff, like a board beneath and above your foot. Wrong. You can create very comfortable lightweight sandals that are still durable.

If you nail or sew a strap into position it is not readily adjustable. If you later want to adjust it the nails must be removed and replaced. You struggle, pry, twist, and yank to remove a well-placed nail and in the process weaken and tear the leather. When you first fit the fixed-strap sandal, it must be too tight to allow for stretch and you can have a lot of agony with heavy latigo digging into your foot for weeks until it stretches. Then the strap gets loose and sloppy and the sandal flaps every time you step. The only reason a sandal slaps and flaps with every step is that it hasn't been made and fitted properly.

The arch-strap designs are not as durable as they appear. They are only as strong as the nails or thread holding them in place. Even if your sole is flexible enough to bend and rise with your arch on every step—which most handmade sandals are not—it still puts enormous strain on the strap and the nails or thread holding them. Sooner or later they will give and fall out or the leather will become weakened and tear and the sandal is finished. This does not happen with a continuous-strap design.

One other thing. Many sandalmakers around the country routinely put in arch supports or they mold the sole into an arch-support shape. It isn't necessary. The padding in the sandal will pack down and conform to the foot and create the natural shape needed by that particular foot.

PATTERNS

Soles

This is the only pattern you need to make for a sandal. It will be used for the topsole, the midsole or sole, the padding, and as a pattern for your strap placement.

Draw the foot as usual (see pages 29–30), being sure to get in between the big toe and the next, and draw the full distance down into the crack between toes so you know the angle at which to place a toe strap. Some people have lots of space between the big toe and the next; draw the full area. A person

with this kind of foot can tolerate design D with two thicknesses of leather between the toes. A normal person couldn't wear that design for an hour.

In making your pattern use a pencil and, as with all the footwear, just follow the shape of the foot. There are a couple of important modifications, naturally.

TOE AREA. Add about ⅜ inch beyond the longest toe and create a nice shape, maintaining at least that distance from the others. You don't need nearly the toe room required for shoes because the toes are free to move. People don't like a sandal too long or with too much sole beyond the toes.

BALL AREA. Stay right on the lines of your foot drawing; don't add or subtract. Don't follow the indentation from the ball toward the toe. Make a nice curving front.

ARCH AREA. After passing the ball, go in ⅛ inch from the lines of the foot drawing to create a snug fit under the arch.

HEEL AREA. At the back of the heel area, *subtract* about ¼ inch from the lines of your foot drawing. This may sound outlandish, but it delivers a much more comfortable sandal. In making your drawing, you drew the Achilles tendon at the heel, which sticks out. The flesh actually touches the floor about ¼ inch or so in from the line of your drawing. If the sandal is any longer than where the foot touches the ground it will feel too big. There will be nothing—as there is in a shoe or moccasin—holding the heel in place, nor any need for it.

One other thing about heels. Even with the back straps there is a lot of heel movement in a sandal. Some people walk on the outer edge of the feet—the hooked-footers—and some on the inner edge of the heel. If you remember to look at the feet and the shoes people are wearing, notice what kind of walker they are and provide for this habit in the pattern. Add to the sides of the heel about a total of ¼ inch, for anybody. Normal walkers get ⅛ inch to each side. Side walkers should have the whole ¼ inch added to the side they favor. This really helps make a good fit.

Straps

PLACEMENT. There are only four basic continuous-strap designs that we use all the time. Uncreative, I readily admit, but highly satisfying in that customers are happy. Each of these designs can be modified at least once, by reducing the number of holes, thus the amount of strapping, from a total of six slots to four slots per sandal. And you do have the option of selecting a strap width.

Style A is the number-one best-all-round, guaranteed, never-fail design. The strap between the toes keeps the foot from going forward, and the straps on the sides hold the sides of the foot. A perfect, classic design.

Many people cannot tolerate the strap between the toes, or they want to wear sandals with socks, or their feet swell. Style B, without the toe strap, runs

a very close second to A and looks good and not too "strappy" on the foot. Style C is a variation of B. D is another classic, good design but can be used only by those with a wide splay between the toes.

Examine the photographs and the drawings and decide. Once you have decided, return to the sole pattern and place the straps on the foot, as you see it on the drawing.

Notice the straps are placed in the obvious fleshy indentations of the foot, in front of and behind the ball of the foot on either side. Avoid placing something on the ball of the foot; it must be free to flex.

Sandal Style A

Important: strap going from slot 4 to slot 5 *must* go under strap going from slots 2 to 3.

Toe strap (4): always start slot at very end of pen line to keep foot from going forward.

Sandal Style B

← indicates direction of pull

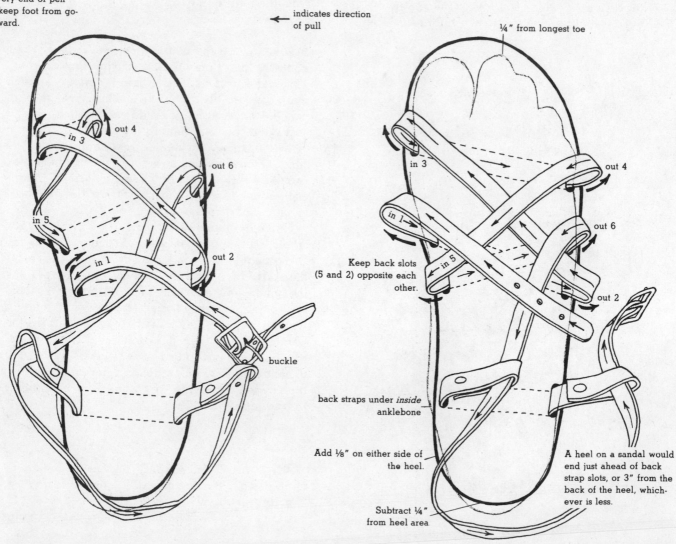

out 4
in 3
out 6
in 5
out 2
in 1
buckle

¼" from longest toe
in 3
out 4
in 1
out 6
in 5
out 2
Keep back slots (5 and 2) opposite each other.
back straps under *inside* anklebone
Add ⅛" on either side of the heel.
Subtract ¼" from heel area
A heel on a sandal would end just ahead of back strap slots, or 3" from the back of the heel, whichever is less.

Avoid strapping or confining in any way the major part of the little toe, any area from the joint bones on up. Sandal latigo is heavy and digs into the toe; it is very painful and annoys people. If you must make an arch strap, avoid giving one to a person with a high arch.

The arrows on the drawings indicate the direction of pull on each strap as it leaves the hole. This is a good thing to remember when you position the straps. Design B, for example, might appear to be contrary to the advice about confining the little toe. However, the direction of pull is away from the toe

and thus it will not pinch it or hurt it. The straps behind the ball (toward the heel) should be as far back as possible so as not to cover the ball. Don't put the straps too far back in the arch area. Keep at least a 3/16-inch distance between the slots so you can place a nail between them and so that the area around each slot retains its strength.

WIDTH. Don't forget about strap width. The same sandal with a 5/8-inch strap will look completely different with a 3/8-inch strap. Small women like 3/8 inch, heavy men can use 5/8 inch, and the general

Sandal Style C (Variation of B)

x = nails placed first
    around stress points

• = remaining nails

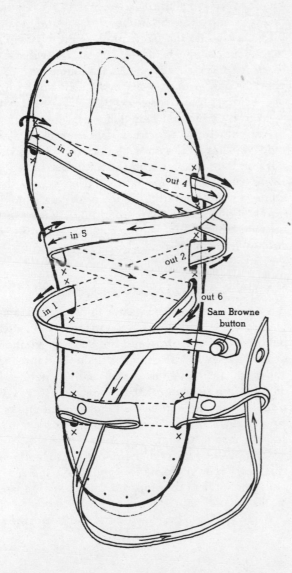

Sandal Style D

This style is best for people who have enough space between their toes that two thicknesses of leather will not bother them.

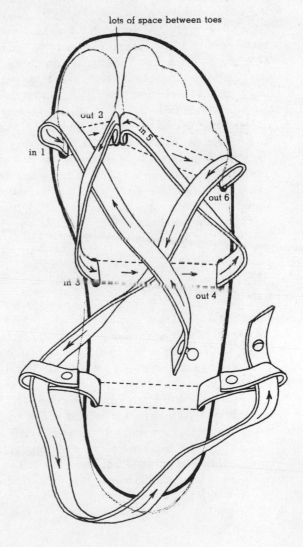

population will use a ½-inch-wide strap. Make a sample strap in all three widths and test them on your foot to see how they look. Some people think ⅜ inch too narrow and ½ inch too thick. Fine, I give them a ⁵⁄₁₆-inch strap. It is hard to believe that ¹⁄₁₆ inch can make a difference, but it does. (But beware and don't put a very heavy soling on a sandal with thin straps—there has to be a balance so that your foot will not receive undue pressure.)

As with shoes, you can select any kind of soling you want, either with the midsole or without. I have made hundreds of sandals with leather soles, nailed, and I switched to the midsole method with a crepe sole only because customers have a decided preference for its comfort. The nails on sandals are not at all obvious—the foot hides most of them and they look perfectly fine—although sewn sandals do look more finished.

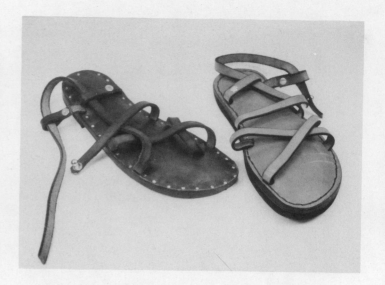

BEFORE ASSEMBLING

Making sandals is really not a living-room activity. It is very helpful to have a worktable big enough to let you lay out straps, dye without being concerned about your rug, and hammer without disturbing the neighbors on the floor below. If you can move to the garage or some other place where you can work more comfortably without worrying about making a mess, it would be a dandy idea.

The construction of soles is identical for sandals and for shoes. Whatever soling, heeling, or wedging you can put on a shoe, you can put on a sandal. The soles of both are finished in the same way. To avoid repetition, the background information and specific procedural instructions for putting the soles together appear in the shoe chapter. Please refer back to pages 59–60 for these detailed explanations.

Cutting

The obvious first step is to cut out all of the pieces. Again, as with shoes, it makes no difference in what order, just so long as all the pieces get cut out and you have the straps and topsole ready to attach to the midsole and padding.

Whatever width strap you've chosen—⅜, ½, or ⅝ inch—set your stripper for that width and peel the straps away from the hide (see page 18). If you cannot afford a separate hide for straps and topsoles, get the heavier-weight hide (9 to 10 ounces) and plan to have a longer breaking-in period. Bark- or vegetable-tanned leather will do, although I prefer latigo. It's fun to use the stripper; just remember

to maintain lots of pressure with your hands so that the leather doesn't wiggle and come out to differing widths (which will also result in a wobbly cutting line for your next strap). The average large person needs a strap about 60 inches long to strap one foot fully—including the back strap. A little excess is a marvelous thing. Of the 60 inches, 12 will be cut away for back straps, so the maximum you really need in one swoop is 50 inches. Leather supply houses do sell all these components precut if you want to try your first pair that way.

Cut your topsoles and midsoles from whatever hide you have. The tops should be from a good portion, the midsoles from a stiff, crummy section. *Don't forget to flip the pattern.* Use a very sharp knife to cut the latigo; it takes effort and time.

When you cut out your padding, don't use the original sole pattern—that would destroy your strap-placement marks.

Transferring Strap Marks and Punching Slots

It is a simple matter to transfer the strap-placement marks from the sole pattern to the topsole. Place the pattern over the topsole and get out your stitcher or a needle or awl. Push the needle through the paper and into the leather to make small punctures indicating the position of the straps, where you will want slots in the leather. Just make small marks on either side of where you want the slot so you will know where to punch.

After pushing through the paper to the leather for one foot, it is a simple matter to flip the pattern over, place it over the other topsole, and make the marks on the second sole.

When you have transferred the marks, get the slot

punch and punch out the slots. These slots should be about 3/16 inch in from the edge of the topsole and at least the same distance apart from each other along the sides. You don't need to measure—just take a few practice punches to develop your eye and learn about your punch, how to get a straight hole where you want it, how big the slot actually is after it is punched, and so on. Don't forget to use soling, rubber or wood, under the topsole as you punch so that the metal will not hit the metal of your anvil.

Edging and Dyeing

This is the fun, creative part of making sandals. Edging (see page 18) simply cleans up the grain edge of the straps so that they look clean and tidy, without any fuzz or nicks on them. Practice with your edger—it doesn't take much pressure; it's just a matter of running the heel of the tool properly along the leather. We'll edge the topsole later.

There are no particular "musts" in dyeing. It is fun. You do not have to dye the straps and topsoles; you can leave them "natural." Or you can burn designs all over them with your woodburner and fill in areas with many colors of dye. It is merely an aesthetic operation.

The traditional way to dye is to get the sandals all one color. We have the greatest demand for light tan, tan, russet, and occasionally dark brown, which are colors sold in the usual places, in various-sized bottles. Fiebings dye is the best; it fades the least and does not powder or rub off. The base of the dye is denatured alcohol, which can be used to dilute it and make it go farther. Start with one color plus black for the edges and work up from there.

Dyes are very messy and 100 percent permanent on clothing and everything else except leather, where they fade. If you spill dye—this takes no effort or imagination—on a table or your driveway, as we did, not even straight hydrochloric acid will remove it. However, the sun will eventually fade it completely away. This fading is a real problem when you have a shop and want things on display in the window. Anything will fade and dry up in direct sunlight and within days look dry and ugly. If you put something on consignment in a shop, make sure it's not put in the window or you'll soon have it on sale—price cut. Oil will revive leather, but not to the original luster.

In applying the dye, get the dauber (a sheepskin ball on a metal stick, which comes with 4-ounce bottles of dye) wet, but not dripping, and run it over the leather. Don't pause in one spot or the result will be splotchy. You'll need to almost soak the leather with dye to get it completely even. There is nothing to it—practice first to see how your leather absorbs the dye and how it handles. Every leather takes the dye differently and looks slightly different. Bark-tanned leather really dries up with dye and needs oil to develop life and patina.

I have always dyed the edges of my straps black. Black hides a multitude of sins and errors and gives the strap a nice look. It is a good optical illusion in minimizing the width of a strap if you want it to look narrower and more delicate than it is. Do the edges after you've colored the strap and be careful to run the dauber just on the edges and not on the strap itself.

ASSEMBLING THE SANDAL

Threading the Straps Through the Topsole

Now the creative part is finished and it is time to start assembling all these various pieces into a sandal. The first step is to thread the straps through the slots of the topsole so they take the shape of the design. It is just a matter of going in one hole and out the other.

The diagrams are numbered according to the slots and the order in which they should be threaded. You are working with one long strap, so it just weaves under and over the topsole, in and out of the holes, starting at 1.

All the designs have an even number of slots, since what goes in must come out. Develop the habit of starting to thread the sandal down at the inside edge of the instep. This is insurance that you will always do it the same way and won't end up with two sandals strapped differently. Start at slot 1: the leather sticking out of this hole will eventually have a buckle or button attached to it, so leave about 7 inches of strap hanging out. Now thread the strap up through, or out of, slot 2, tighten it across the bottom of the topsole, and thread it down through, or in, slot 3, leaving enough room for what you guess to be the foot size, and so on, following the numbered order on the diagram. If the sandals are for you, you can fit them to your foot after threading so you'll know almost exactly how much strapping will be excess. If they are for someone else, just make a guesstimate. The only important thing is to have enough strap to encase the foot, and have the straps tight against the bottom of the topsole. Unless you are like the princess and the pea, you'll never feel these straps under your foot because of the padding. If you were not using padding, you would feel the straps and have to take elaborate measures to bury them.

Once the sandal is threaded and you feel you have enough to cover the foot, lop 12 inches off the end for the back strap. I wait to lop until I know for sure that I'm going to have enough. Then thread the back strap (that extra foot) in one side and out the other at the heel, leaving it loose until you can fit it under the anklebone.

Attaching Topsoles to Midsoles

Most of this process is exactly the same as when making shoes. You must glue the topsoles to the midsoles and then sew or nail them together (see page 60).

GLUING. Spread the ½-inch margin of glue around the edges, as usual. Be careful to get as little glue as possible around the slots or on the straps of the topsole, or you will have problems moving the straps later on.

Because you have two stiff pieces of latigo, plus padding and straps between, there can be a lot of resistance in getting the pieces to stay together. It may take considerable effort and some hammering to get the edges down; try not to strike the straps with the hammer in your efforts.

SEWING OR NAILING.   Sewing sandals is exactly the same as sewing shoes, using a stitcher and thread.

If you have decided to nail, gather together your tack hammer, nails, and anvil, and get to work. It really is very easy.

I use plenty of shoemaking nails. There is that strong pressure exerted by the padding inside until it packs down. Occasionally the latigo is so oily and the pressure so strong that the two soles pull apart. The only thing to do is get some nails in the stress points. The stress points on your sandals are on either side of each slot—marked with an X. I put nails there first to make everything stay down and in place. In place means the two edges—topsole and midsole or sole—even with each other. This frequently requires tremendous pressure with your left hand while you position and hammer the nails with your right. If the pieces are not exactly lined up, if the edge of the topsole draws away from the midsole or sole, don't be overly concerned about it. Keep your nails right beside you so you can grab one quickly. Be sure to keep checking to see if they have gone through to the underside and clinched.

After placing nails in the stress points, put in the remainder of the nails around the edge, trying to

maintain an even distance between them. Just make it look uniform. There is no rigid requirement about the number of nails needed; they should be about ½ or ⅝ inch apart, and the head of the nail should be at least ⅛ inch from the edge, as shown in the illustration (page 88). You'll need room to sand and grind away the edge without hitting a nail.

Applying the Sole

Once the sandal is together you have only to apply the sole and finish up that part the same way you do the shoes, adding heels or wedges or whatever you've planned and then fitting it to the foot.

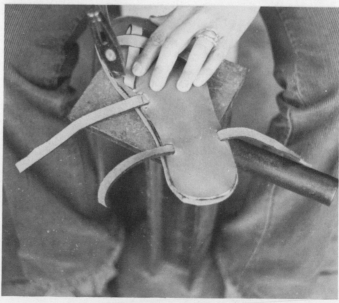

When you sand the edges of the sole, make sure you keep the straps out of the way of the sander; they are easily nicked, as are your knuckles.

FITTING THE SANDAL TO THE FOOT

If your customer is around for the fitting of the buckle and the back straps, it makes the fitting that much more accurate, but you can also do it by guessing.

Have the person put the sandal on and stand up. Once again you are in for your dog's-eye view of the world, so prepare to crawl.

The straps should be tightened on the foot. If you didn't apply too much glue around the slots they should move fairly easily. Pull and yank to get them in motion. It helps to have the person standing so his weight holds the sandal in place. Don't be afraid of breaking the strap or tearing the leather—you can't pull too hard. Nothing can be harmed now. Just pull from both ends of the strap and get the strapping tight on the foot—it will stretch out in seconds. Check to see that the strap (from slot 6) going around the ankle will be long enough to go around and attach to a buckle or button.

Measure where the buckle will fall on the instep and mark that spot on the leather. You initially allotted 7 inches of leather for the buckle on the strap coming out of slot 1, and you should have more than enough to cover the instep with about 1½ inches of excess to attach the buckle, or no excess if you've chosen the button.

At this point you have about 4 inches of leather, at least, coming out of the back slots. Some of this is excess and will be cut away. The purpose of this back piece of leather is to loop over and hold the sandal strapping down under the anklebones, where it circles the heel. The height of this strap should be measured so that it falls right under the bump of the outside anklebone. Probably your measurement will fall somewhere between 2 inches and 2½ inches from the topsole. The straps should not rub the bone. Just hold the strapping up to the point under the bone, make a mark on the inside of the leather, take the sandals off, and repair to your anvil to set the buckle and finish and set the back straps.

After measuring the height for the back straps, fold the leather over to form a loop through which the sandal strapping will pass and which will hold it down. You must now determine how much leather you will need beyond that mark to form the loop and rivet the end to the lower part of the back strap. Generally you will need a minimum of 1¼ inches

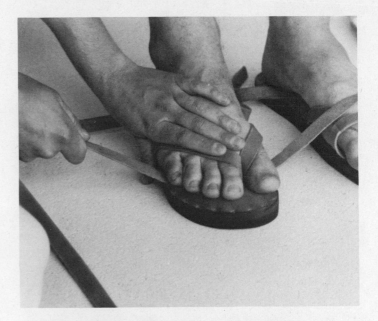

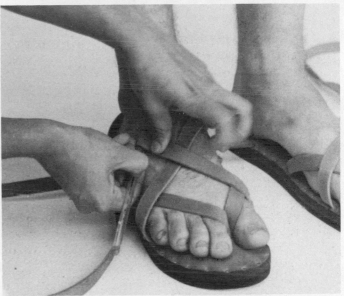

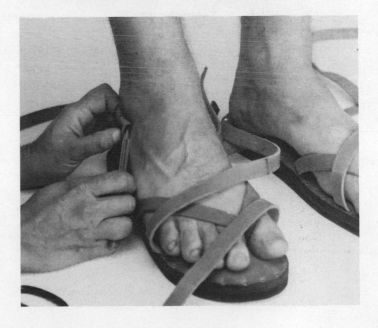

of leather beyond the height you marked for the strap.

Some people like to wear the buckle at the heel. Since this is a difficult place to reach, I suspect they never bother to unbuckle it, but slip off the strap, which means it is too loose. But if you want to please everybody's whim, make the loop big enough for a buckle to pass through.

Fold the leather over at the mark, put the strapping through the loop you've created to make certain it will move through easily, and pinch the end of the loop to determine the position of your rivet. Then cut off the excess, punch the rivet holes, and rivet.

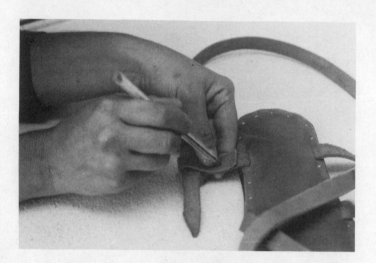

If your leather is heavy, it is sensible to skive it down where the back strap is riveted. Skiving is the process whereby you shave or thin the leather. Latigo is easy to skive; soft leather is difficult to skive. Just use a sharp utility knife and whittle away a little of the thickness at the end so that it doesn't rub the foot. You can do this where you join the buckle too.

Attach the buckle or button (see pages 25–6) and return the sandal to the foot. There are many methods of attaching the straps other than the buckle or button, but either they do not hold the leather securely or they are too bothersome to reattach every time the sandals are worn and thus are left permanently closed with the result that the leather stretches and you get a loose and floppy fit.

Once the sandal is back on the foot, you need only match up the buckle or button with the other end of the strap, punch holes, and attach. Line up the strap with the buckle and mark with a pen where the first hole will go. Punch the hole and then several more going away from the end of the strap (because there will be so much stretch) and buckle

the strap. Now cut off the excess strapping that hangs out of the buckle. Don't cut it before this moment, because you can have made a mistake.

You are finished, and everyone should be all smiles. Have the customer hop around the room, do a merry jig, and admire your work. Notice the fit, how it stays on the foot, whether there is any slap-slap in the back. Don't forget in all the excitement to collect your money, if these aren't a gift or for yourself.

If the sandal rubs anywhere on the foot, you can apply a little oil next to where it is rubbing and smooth and soften the leather. If the customer thinks the color too dark, remind him that all leather dyes

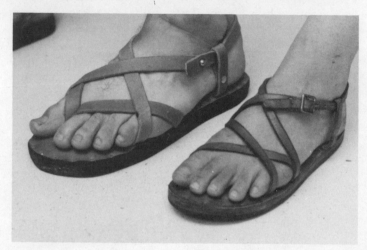

fade. If he thinks the color too light, remind him that the dirt in the air and the oils will darken it. Be sure to explain how the spiral strap works so he can tighten it himself at home.

You should be very pleased with yourself. It is such fun to make something nice for someone. But don't expect the same person back for another pair for a long time; these sandals will last and last.

SANDAL VARIATIONS

Leather Thongs

If you like thongs you can slip-slap around in and kick off when you want to, they can easily be put together the morning before the picnic and will last for at least one entire season.

I've made two designs. Both consist of one strap, a topsole, and a sole, and the whole thing is glued together. Very, very simple.

Style 1, in which the ends of the strap begin and end underneath the topsole at the toe, is the more popular. But be aware that since both pieces of leather must go between the toes this can be uncomfortable for many. Style 2 rivets one strap to the other just back of the toe and thus eliminates the double thickness, plus providing a means for easy adjustment when stretch occurs.

Style 1 can be adjusted only by cutting away a portion of strapping beneath the arch and resewing it.

Draw the foot as usual and make the pattern for sandal soles as usual, except add about ⅛ inch to each side of the heel area because there is nothing holding the heel in place and it will move around. There will be three slots: one between the big toe and the next and two under the back portion of the

arch, about ½ inch in front of the inside anklebone.

Cut out topsoles in latigo and one strap about 4 feet long which will serve to strap both thongs. The strap should be about ½ or ⅝ inch wide. Cut out two crepe soles large enough so that you have the extra margin of safety.

Punch the slots. Style 1 gets a double slot between the toes. Punch the rear slots about ½ inch in from the edge of the topsole so you will be able to glue the edges together completely around the thong.

Thread the strap through the slots. Style 1 should fit very tight to the foot, and the ends of the strap

Leather Thongs

Style 1

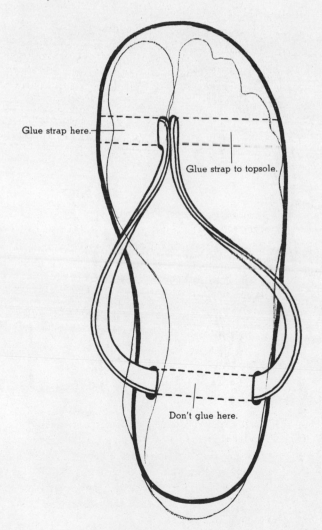

Glue strap here.

Glue strap to topsole.

Don't glue here.

Style 2

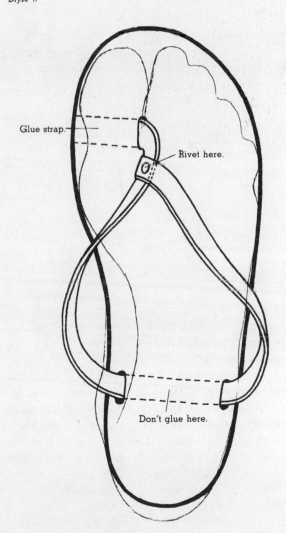

Glue strap.

Rivet here.

Don't glue here.

should be glued to the bottom of the topsole and extend beyond the edge of the leather under the toes. Style 2 is threaded; one end is glued to the topsole under the toe and the other end left loose for fitting later.

Then everything is glued *except:* Do not put glue on the area of the sole or the strap that goes under the arch. Leaving this unglued will permit the strap to move and be adjustable. Glue both soles (four pieces), let them dry, and put them together. Then sand and burnish the edges.

To fit style 2, put it on and pull the strap as tight as possible. Wrap the loose end so that it crosses the other right by the big toe, mark where the pieces cross, punch rivet holes, and rivet. Cut off the excess. When the leather stretches, remove the rivet, tighten the strap, and rerivet.

Arch-Strap Designs

Arch-strap and fixed-strap designs are easy. They should be fitted to the foot as tight as you can stand, so they can stretch and not be terribly loose and sloppy.

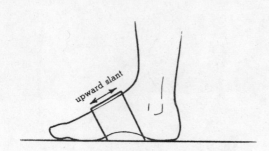

To make them, draw the foot as usual, making sure to draw inside the arch. Make your sole pattern as usual. Arch-strap widths vary from 1½ inches to 1¾ inches, depending on taste or size. The important thing to remember is that the strap must be angled to follow the upward slant of the instep of the foot. To accomplish this you must cut the slots for the strap at least ¼ inch longer than the width of the strap you are using. Thus a slot for a 1½-inch strap must be 1¾ inches and for a 1¾-inch strap, 2 inches. This will give you room to angle the strap so it follows the contours of the foot.

As a general rule, you will need aproximately 10 to 12 inches of the wide leather pieces for the arch strap. Measure your foot. Usually you will fix the arch side of the strap into position before doing the

fitting. It should be glued and nailed in, under the leather and arch. The outside strap is tucked down through the outside slot and brought out between the edges of the leather and sole. After the sandal is completely nailed, fit it to the foot, making sure the strap is angled correctly over your instep and is tight. Mark the tightened position with a pen, nail the strap into place, and cut away the excess. When it eventually stretches, pull out the nails and tighten until the sandal is comfortable, not too tight, because although the leather will continue to stretch, the stretch the second time won't be as significant.

The toe strap, if you want to use one, should be positioned as in the illustration and fitted around the widest part of the toe. If you put the two toe slots opposite each other there will be too much pressure on the toe and it will be painful.

Sandal with Arch Strap

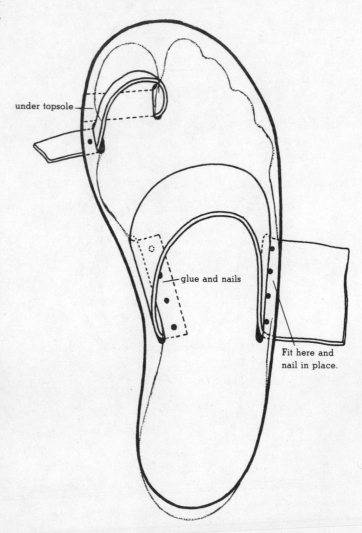

Suppliers

Many, many places all over the country sell leather, tools, and other supplies you will need. The ones listed are the ones I am familiar with and have dealt with. Be sure to look in your Yellow Pages, or those of the nearest large city, under "Leather," "Shoe Findings," and "Upholstery Supplies." Or ask the owner of your local shoe repair shop whom he deals with. (Do be tactful—he might think you are competition and be unwilling to disclose his sources.)

Several places will say wholesale only. These are generally the better places to deal with; they seem to have more to choose from. "Wholesale" (at least in this business) does not mean you must buy in great quantity. It seems to mean that they want you to have a wholesale or resale tax number, which gives you entrée into places that otherwise would not deal with you. To get this number in most states you merely have to file with the state. What you file is a declaration that you are in business, but the states I have dealt with don't seem to care whether you are going to be doing $20 worth of business a year or a great deal more. They are concerned about collecting every nickel of sales tax money they can and are delighted to have whatever you contribute. And if you don't sell anything—well, lots of small businesses don't sell anything.

If you write to any of these places and must order by mail, be sure to get samples of the leather they carry.

LEATHER

Berman Leather Co.
147 South Street
Boston, Massachusetts 02130

Very big concern; they carry most of the leathers you'll need and are set up to do mail order.

Goliger Leather Co. Inc.
1734 Maple Street
Los Angeles, California 90015

Wholesale.

A. C. Lawrence Tanning Company
Winchester, New Hampshire 03470

Tanners of sheepskin.

Leathercrafters Supply Company
25 Great Jones Street
New York, New York 10003

Mail-order catalog $1.50.

Macpherson Bros.
730 Polk Street
San Francisco, California 94109

Mail order.

Sav-Mor Leather & Supply
1409 Los Angeles Street
Los Angeles, California 90015

Very fair, well-stocked place.

M. Siegel Company, Inc.
186 South Street
Boston, Massachusetts 02111

Nice outfit also; will do mail order.

Sierra Pine Tanning Company
The Hide Out
3001 Sierra Pine Boulevard
Vernon, California 90058

Nice people—ask for Tom—very superior sheepskins.

TOOLS

C. S. Osborn & Company
Harrison, New Jersey 07029

Manufacturers of Osborn Tools. They will not sell to you, but will supply a list of their distributors, which includes leather suppliers throughout the country.

THREAD

Western Filament, Inc.
Glendale, California 91204

Manufacturers only. Ask for a list of distributors, or one in your area

    Thread: 500 yards
    MF6   Tape Nylon
              Mil-T 43435 A Type 1
              Size 3, Finish B

PADDING

Sears (Catalog: Upholstery Supplies)
Polyurethane Foam
Extra-Firm Serosuper—Cat. #24 H 87831P

Thos. J. Anthoine Co.
561 Pleasant Street
Lewiston, Maine 04240

Manufacturers; will sell to public. They also manufacture foam used by shoe companies to insulate boots for below-zero temperatures. I haven't tried it yet, but am sure it could be used between two layers of leather.

Please drop me a line in Sedgwick, Maine 04676, for any leather or supplies you may need. I'll be happy to help you.

Index

A Note About the Author

Christine Lewis Clark was born in Pittsburgh, Pennsylvania, and raised in Miami, Florida. She has degrees in English and human behavior and has worked as an executive secretary, an English teacher, a correctional officer, and since 1971 has been in the shoemaking business—making and selling shoes and teaching the craft. A resident of Sedgwick, Maine, Ms. Clark has been busy lately not only with her shoe business and this book, but also restoring her house, which was originally used as a shoemaking shop by her great-great-great-grandfather.

A Note About the Type

The text of this book was set, via computer-driven cathode
ray tube, in Stymie, originally a linotype face designed
by M. F. Benton for American Type Founders in 1931.
Its even weight and round, open letters make it a
particularly readable face.

Composed by CompuComp Corporation, Hoboken,
New Jersey. Printed and bound by Murray Printing Co.,
Forge Village, Massachusetts.

Line illustrations by Virginia Tan.
Photographs by Christine Lewis Clark, James Clark,
Martha Kaplan, and Susan Mitchell.
Typography and binding design by Susan Mitchell.